BANANA-GRAMS!®

THE OFFICIAL BOOK

BY JOE EDLEY

AND
THE CREATORS
OF

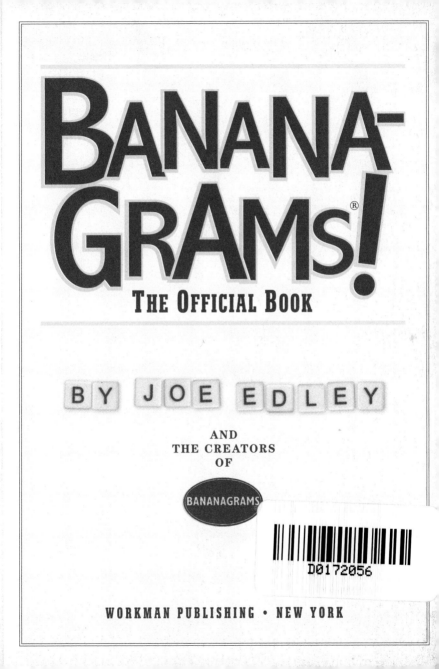

BANANAGRAMS

WORKMAN PUBLISHING • NEW YORK

Copyright © 2009 Bananagrams

Puzzles by Joe Edley

All rights reserved. No portion of this book may be repro-
duced—mechanically, electronically, or by any other means,
including photocopying—without written permission of the
publisher. Published simultaneously in Canada by Thomas
Allen & Son Limited.

Library of Congress Cataloging-in-Publication Data is available

ISBN 978-0-7611-5635-2

Workman books are available at special discounts when
purchased in bulk for premiums and sales promotions as well
as for fund-raising or educational use. Special editions or book
excerpts also can be created to specification. For details, con-
tact the Special Sales Director at the address below.

Design by Rae Ann Spitzenberger

Bananagrams® is a trademark owned by Abe Nathanson
doing business as Bananagrams, registered U.S. Patent and
Trademark Office.

Photograph © Olga Shelego

WORKMAN PUBLISHING COMPANY, INC.
225 Varick Street
New York, NY 10014-4381
www.workman.com

Printed in the United States of America
First printing August 2009

10 9 8 7 6 5 4

WELCOME TO

B A N A N A G R A M S

THE OFFICIAL BOOK

W ord-game fanatics: get ready for something totally new—and totally bananas! People everywhere have fallen for **Bananagrams**, the addictive craze that started as a simple idea: "An **anagram** game that is so fast it will drive you **bananas**!" And why not? It's amazingly fun and easy to play: you pick lettered tiles and create a grid of connecting and inter-secting words as fast as you can.

It all began one summer when three generations of our family were vacationing together on the beach. We wanted a game that everybody—no matter their age—could enjoy. After marathon sessions playing and experimenting with various permutations of word games, we ended up inventing Bananagrams. Our family was hooked—and so we decided to share our new creation with everyone. The next thing we knew the game was named Game of the Year. Not bad for a rainy-day invention.

Now we've taken it to the next level with *Bananagrams! The Official Book*. Jam-packed with hundreds of puzzles, this book brings the brain-twisting wordplay of the game onto the page so you can take it anywhere—in the car, on the train, even in the bathtub. We've worked together with Joe Edley to create this collection of endlessly entertaining puzzles. Joe, the only three-time National Scrabble Champion in history, has carefully crafted these smart puzzles using his unparalleled anagram-ming skills. This book captures the same grid-building fun of the game, but it also offers tons of new and exciting challenges that will thrill solvers of all stripes. So even if you've never grabbed a tile from a Bananagrams pouch, you're sure to find these puzzles very a-peel-ing!

HOW TO PLAY

Like the game, the puzzles in *Bananagrams! The Official Book* are fast and fun. In all, there are seven puzzle categories—some offer one big grid-building challenge, while others feature a group of shorter problems to solve more quickly. Each puzzle is ranked by difficulty, ranging from one banana (easy) to four bananas (very hard).

The farther you go into the book the harder the puzzles get, so dive in wherever you feel comfortable. If you're a beginner, you might want to try solving the puzzles with a pencil, since you may need to cross off tiles more than once. But if you're feeling brave, grab a pen!

All of the puzzles can be solved using common English words that appear in any standard dictionary. Just for fun, we've included a list of **Weords** (weird words!) on the next page which we've compiled especially for Bananagrams players. This list features fun and unusual words that can come in very handy when you get stuck solving a puzzle. Flip to the back of the book for the answer key which starts on page 268. You'll notice that some of the puzzles have multiple solutions; in these cases the key gives only one of the many possible answers. If you find a different one, good for you— you've earned some bragging rights!

We hope you'll dive right in and start solving. Have fun and don't be surprised if these puzzles drive you bananas!

Abe, Rena, Ava and Aaron Nathanson
The creators of Bananagrams

**These WEORDS (weird words!) are strange and useful
words that can help you be a better Bananagrammer. Have
a bunch full of A s and O s and U s? Or maybe you need the
perfect 3-letter word that starts with Y to finish your grid?
These lists of handy and unusual words can help get you out
of many a Bananagrams jam!**

2-LETTER WORDS

AA	AY	ES	IT	NE	OY	UP
AB	BA	ET	JO	NO	PA	US
AD	BE	EX	KA	NU	PE	UT
AE	BI	FA	KI	OD	PI	WE
AG	BO	FE	LA	OE	QI	WO
AH	BY	GO	LI	OF	RE	XI
AI	DE	HA	LO	OH	SH	XU
AL	DO	HE	MA	OI	SI	YA
AM	ED	HI	ME	OM	SO	YE
AN	EF	HM	MI	ON	TA	YO
AR	EH	HO	MM	OP	TI	ZA
AS	EL	ID	MO	OR	TO	
AT	EM	IF	MU	OS	UH	
AW	EN	IN	MY	OW	UM	
AX	ER	IS	NA	OX	UN	

3-LETTER WORDS

AAH	ACT	AGA	AID	ALA	AMA	ANI
AAL	ADD	AGE	AIL	ALB	AMI	ANT
AAS	ADO	AGO	AIM	ALE	AMP	ANY
ABA	ADS	AGS	AIN	ALL	AMU	APE
ABS	ADZ	AHA	AIR	ALP	ANA	APO
ABY	AFF	AHI	AIS	ALS	AND	APP
ACE	AFT	AHS	AIT	ALT	ANE	APT

1

ARB	BED	BUY	CUP	DOM	EMS	FIB
ARC	BEE	BYE	CUR	DON	EMU	FID
ARE	BEG	BYS	CUT	DOR	END	FIE
ARF	BEL	CAB	CWM	DOS	ENG	FIG
ARK	BEN	CAD	DAB	DOT	ENS	FIL
ARM	BES	CAM	DAD	DOW	EON	FIN
ARS	BET	CAN	DAG	DRY	ERA	FIR
ART	BEY	CAP	DAH	DUB	ERE	FIT
ASH	BIB	CAR	DAK	DUD	ERG	FIX
ASK	BID	CAT	DAL	DUE	ERN	FIZ
ASP	BIG	CAW	DAM	DUG	ERR	FLU
ASS	BIN	CAY	DAN	DUH	ERS	FLY
ATE	BIO	CEE	DAP	DUN	ESS	FOB
ATT	BIS	CEL	DAW	DUO	ETA	FOE
AUK	BIT	CEP	DAY	DUP	ETH	FOG
AVA	BIZ	CHI	DEB	DYE	EVE	FOH
AVE	BOA	CIG	DEE	EAR	EWE	FON
AVO	BOB	CIS	DEF	EAT	EYE	FOP
AWA	BOD	COB	DEL	EAU	FAB	FOR
AWE	BOG	COD	DEN	EBB	FAD	FOU
AWL	BOO	COG	DEV	ECU	FAN	FOX
AWN	BOP	COL	DEW	EDH	FAR	FOY
AXE	BOS	CON	DEX	EDS	FAS	FRO
AYE	BOT	COO	DEY	EEK	FAT	FRY
AYS	BOW	COP	DIB	EEL	FAX	FUB
AZO	BOX	COR	DID	EFF	FAY	FUD
BAA	BOY	COS	DIE	EFS	FED	FUG
BAD	BRA	COT	DIF	EFT	FEE	FUN
BAG	BRO	COW	DIG	EGG	FEH	FUR
BAH	BRR	COX	DIM	EGO	FEM	GAB
BAL	BUB	COY	DIN	EKE	FEN	GAD
BAM	BUD	COZ	DIP	ELD	FER	GAE
BAN	BUG	CRU	DIS	ELF	FES	GAG
BAP	BUM	CRY	DIT	ELK	FET	GAL
BAR	BUN	CUB	DOC	ELL	FEU	GAM
BAS	BUR	CUD	DOE	ELM	FEW	GAN
BAT	BUS	CUE	DOG	ELS	FEY	GAP
BAY	BUT	CUM	DOL	EME	FEZ	GAR

Did You Know?

• Contrary to popular belief, bananas do not grow on trees. They're actually the fruit of a giant herb plant which can grow to be 20 feet high.

• Bananas are technically classified as berries. They are also distant cousins to ginger, turmeric and cardamom.

• Bananas grow in hanging clusters known as hands. Each hand consists of 10 to 20 bananas, which are called fingers.

				HOT	JEE	KOA
				HOW	JET	KOB
				HOY	JEU	KOI
				HUB	JEW	KOP
				HUE	JIB	KOR
				HUG	JIG	KOS
				HUH	JIN	KUE
				HUM	JOB	KYE
				HUN	JOE	LAB
				HUP	JOG	LAC
				HUT	JOT	LAD
				HYP	JOW	LAG
				ICE	JOY	LAM
				ICH	JUG	LAP
				ICK	JUN	LAR
				ICY	JUS	LAS
				IDS	JUT	LAT
				IFF	KAB	LAV
				IFS	KAE	LAW
				IGG	KAF	LAX
GAS	GNU	HAE	HEW	ILK	KAS	LAY
GAT	GOA	HAG	HEX	ILL	KAT	LEA
GAY	GOB	HAH	HEY	IMP	KAY	LED
GED	GOD	HAJ	HIC	INK	KEA	LEE
GEE	GOO	HAM	HID	INN	KEF	LEG
GEL	GOR	HAO	HIE	INS	KEG	LEI
GEM	GOS	HAP	HIM	ION	KEN	LEK
GEN	GOT	HAS	HIN	IRE	KEP	LES
GET	GOX	HAT	HIP	IRK	KEX	LET
GEY	GUL	HAW	HIS	ISM	KEY	LEU
GHI	GUM	HAY	HIT	ITS	KHI	LEV
GIB	GUN	HEH	HMM	IVY	KID	LEX
GID	GUT	HEM	HOB	JAB	KIF	LEY
GIE	GUV	HEN	HOD	JAG	KIN	LIB
GIG	GUY	HEP	HOE	JAM	KIP	LID
GIN	GYM	HER	HOG	JAR	KIR	LIE
GIP	GYP	HES	HON	JAW	KIS	LIN
GIT	HAD	HET	HOP	JAY	KIT	LIP

LIS	MIL	NET	OHM	OPS	OXO	PEA
LIT	MIM	NEW	OHO	OPT	OXY	PEC
LOB	MIR	NIB	OHS	ORA	PAC	PED
LOG	MIS	NIL	OIL	ORB	PAD	PEE
LOO	MIX	NIM	OKA	ORC	PAH	PEG
LOP	MOA	NIP	OKE	ORE	PAL	PEH
LOT	MOB	NIT	OLD	ORS	PAM	PEN
LOW	MOC	NIX	OLE	OSE	PAN	PEP
LOX	MOD	NOB	OMS	OUD	PAP	PER
LUG	MOG	NOD	ONE	OUR	PAR	PES
LUM	MOL	NOG	ONO	OUT	PAS	PET
LUV	MOM	NOH	ONS	OVA	PAT	PEW
LUX	MON	NOM	OOH	OWE	PAW	PHI
LYE	MOO	NOO	OOT	OWL	PAX	PHT
MAC	MOP	NOR	OPE	OWN	PAY	PIA
MAD	MOR	NOS				
MAE	MOS	NOT				
MAG	MOT	NOW				
MAN	MOW	NTH				
MAP	MUD	NUB				
MAR	MUG	NUN				
MAS	MUM	NUS				
MAT	MUN	NUT				
MAW	MUS	OAF				
MAX	MUT	OAK				
MAY	MYC	OAR				
MED	NAB	OAT				
MEG	NAE	OBA				
MEL	NAG	OBE				
MEM	NAH	OBI				
MEN	NAM	OCA				
MET	NAN	ODA				
MEW	NAP	ODD				
MHO	NAW	ODE				
MIB	NAY	ODS				
MIC	NEB	OES				
MID	NEE	OFF				
MIG	NEG	OFT				

Did You Know?

• Bananas are the most popular fruit in the United States. As many as two million tons of bananas are imported into the country each year.

• Americans eat an average of 28 pounds of bananas per person each year. That breaks down to about 112 bananas for every person.

• There are hundreds of varieties of bananas. The most commonly eaten type in the U.S. is the Cavendish. It's also referred to as the dessert banana, because it is quite soft and sweet compared to many other varieties.

PIC	RAD	ROE	SHY	TAB	TON	VAR
PIE	RAG	ROM	SIB	TAD	TOO	VAS
PIG	RAH	ROT	SIC	TAE	TOP	VAT
PIN	RAI	ROW	SIM	TAG	TOR	VAU
PIP	RAJ	RUB	SIN	TAJ	TOT	VAV
PIS	RAM	RUE	SIP	TAM	TOW	VAW
PIT	RAN	RUG	SIR	TAN	TOY	VEE
PIU	RAP	RUM	SIS	TAO	TRY	VEG
PIX	RAS	RUN	SIT	TAP	TSK	VET
PLY	RAT	RUT	SIX	TAR	TUB	VEX
POD	RAW	RYA	SKA	TAS	TUG	VIA
POH	RAX	RYE	SKI	TAT	TUI	VID
POI	RAY	SAB	SKY	TAU	TUN	VIE
POL	REB	SAC	SLY	TAV	TUP	VIG
POO	REC	SAD	SOB	TAW	TUT	VIM
POP	RED	SAE	SOD	TAX	TUX	VIS
POT	REE	SAG	SOL	TEA	TWA	VOE
POW	REF	SAL	SOM	TED	TWO	VOW
POX	REG	SAP	SON	TEE	TYE	VOX
PRO	REI	SAT	SOP	TEG	UDO	VUG
PRY	REM	SAU	SOS	TEL	UGH	VUM
PSI	REP	SAW	SOT	TEN	UKE	WAB
PST	RES	SAX	SOU	TET	ULU	WAD
PUB	RET	SAY	SOW	TEW	UMM	WAE
PUD	REV	SEA	SOX	THE	UMP	WAG
PUG	REX	SEC	SOY	THO	UNS	WAN
PUL	RHO	SEE	SPA	THY	UPO	WAP
PUN	RIA	SEG	SPY	TIC	UPS	WAR
PUP	RIB	SEI	SRI	TIE	URB	WAS
PUR	RID	SEL	STY	TIL	URD	WAT
PUS	RIF	SEN	SUB	TIN	URN	WAW
PUT	RIG	SER	SUE	TIP	URP	WAX
PYA	RIM	SET	SUK	TIS	USE	WAY
PYE	RIN	SEW	SUM	TIT	UTA	WEB
PYX	RIP	SEX	SUN	TOD	UTE	WED
QAT	ROB	SHA	SUP	TOE	UTS	WEE
QIS	ROC	SHE	SUQ	TOG	VAC	WEN
QUA	ROD	SHH	SYN	TOM	VAN	WET

WHA	WOK	WYN	YAY	YIP	YUM	ZEP
WHO	WON	XIS	YEA	YOB	YUP	ZIG
WHY	WOO	YAG	YEH	YOD	ZAG	ZIN
WIG	WOS	YAH	YEN	YOK	ZAP	ZIP
WIN	WOT	YAK	YEP	YOM	ZAS	ZIT
WIS	WOW	YAM	YES	YON	ZAX	ZOA
WIT	WRY	YAP	YET	YOU	ZED	ZOO
WIZ	WUD	YAR	YEW	YOW	ZEE	ZUZ
WOE	WYE	YAW	YIN	YUK	ZEK	ZZZ

WORDS WITH A LOT OF VOWELS

AA	AUDIO	LOUIE	OIDIA	ROUE
AALII	AURA	LUAU	OLEA	TOEA
ADIEU	AURAE	MEOU	OLEO	UNAI
AE	AUREI	MIAOU	OLIO	UNAU
AECIA	AUTO	MOUE	OORIE	URAEI
AEON	AWEE	OBIA	OOZE	UREA
AERIE	BEAU	OBOE	OURIE	UVEA
AERO	CIAO	OE	OUZO	ZOEA
AGEE	EASE	OGEE	QUAI	ZOEAE
AGIO	EAU	OI	QUEUE	
AGUE	EAUX			
AI	EAVE			
AIDE	EERIE			
AIOLI	EIDE			
AJEE	EMEU			
AKEE	EPEE			
ALAE	ETUI			
ALEE	EURO			
ALOE	IDEA			
AMIA	ILEA			
AMIE	ILIA			
ANOA	INIA			
AQUA	IOTA			
AREA	IXIA			
ARIA	JIAO			
ASEA	LIEU			

Did You Know?

• Bananas are an excellent source of vitamin C, vitamin B$_6$, potassium, iron and fiber. They are also virtually sodium, fat and cholesterol free.

• Bananas aren't just good for your body; they're also good for your spirit. Eating a banana can actually cheer you up—they contain chemicals which help regulate your mood.

WORDS WITH NO VOWELS

BRR
BY(S)
CRWTH
CRY
CRYPT(S)
CWM
CYST(S)
DRY(S)
DRYLY
FLY
FLYBY(S)
FLYSCH
FRY
GHYLL(S)
GLYCYL(S)
GLYPH(S)
GYM(S)
GYP(S)
GYPSY
HM

HMM
HYMN(S)
HYP(S)
LYMPH(S)
LYNCH
LYNX
MM
MY
MYC(S)
MYRRH(S)
MYTH(S)
MYTHY
NTH
NYMPH(S)
PLY
PRY
PST
PSYCH(S)
PYGMY
PYX

RHYTHM(S)
RYND(S)
SCRY
SH
SHY
SHYLY
SKY
SLY
SLYLY
SPRY
SPRYLY
SPY
STY
STYMY
SYLPH(S)
SYLPHY
SYN
SYNC(S)
SYNCH(S)
SYNTH(S)

SYPH(S)
SYZYGY
THY
THYMY
TRY
TRYST(S)
TSK
TYPP(S)
TYPY
WHY(S)
WRY
WRYLY
WYCH
WYN(S)
WYND(S)
WYNN(S)
XYLYL(S)
XYST(S)
ZZZ

Q WORDS WITH NO U

FAQIR(S)
MBAQANGA(S)
QABALA(S)
QABALAH(S)
QADI(S)
QAID(S)

QANAT(S)
QAT(S)
QI
QINDAR(S)
QINDARKA
QINTAR(S)

QIS
QOPH(S)
QWERTY(S)
SHEQALIM
SHEQEL(S)
TRANQ(S)

BANANA-GRAMS!

THE PUZZLES

GO BANANAS!

LEVEL

Use all 21 tiles in this bunch to create a collection of connecting and intersecting common words in the grid below. The words may be horizontal or vertical, reading left to right or top to bottom.

Each of the two-letter groups below may be extended both on the right and the left to form a six-letter word. Drawing from the tiles directly above each group, fill in the blanks to find the words as quickly as you can.

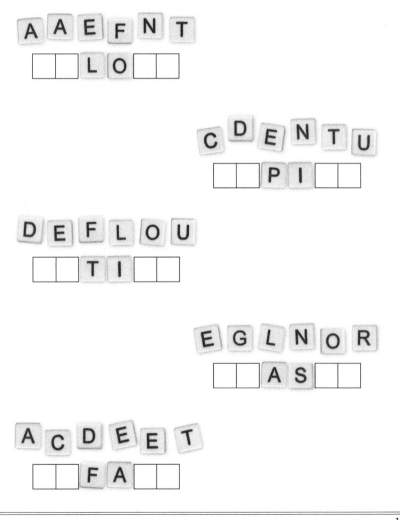

A A E F N T

☐ ☐ L O ☐ ☐

C D E N T U

☐ ☐ P I ☐ ☐

D E F L O U

☐ ☐ T I ☐ ☐

E G L N O R

☐ ☐ A S ☐ ☐

A C D E E T

☐ ☐ F A ☐ ☐

BANANA SPLITS

LEVEL

For each of the three words below, change one letter to an O **and then rearrange the letters to spell a type of animal.**

G A T E

☐ ☐ ☐ ☐

L I N E

☐ ☐ ☐ ☐

S H A R E

☐ ☐ ☐ ☐ ☐

For each of the three words below, change one letter to an F **and then rearrange the letters to spell a part of the body.**

C A V E

☐ ☐ ☐ ☐

L A C Y

☐ ☐ ☐ ☐

T O O K

☐ ☐ ☐ ☐

14

Replace each of the question marks below with one of the vowels A , E , I , O **or** U **and then rearrange the letters to form a common word. Each vowel will be used only once.**

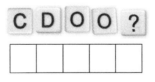

BANANA TREES

LEVEL

Use this bunch of 15 tiles to fill in each of the four grids below. To get you started, a few tiles from the bunch have been placed in each grid. Using the remaining tiles in the bunch, find words that complete each grid.

A F E Y T N W V
E I N W U V J

1.

2.

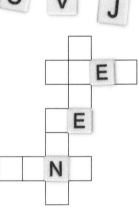

3.

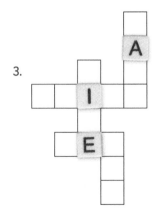

4.

Use the 15 tiles in this bunch to create words that fit into the grids below. You will reuse this bunch for each of the four grids. The BANANA BITES provide hints to help you solve each grid.

LEVEL

A I U E G P T V
E O A D L R N

1. **BANANA BITE:** One word means "to steer clear."

2. **BANANA BITE:** One word is a body of water.

3. **BANANA BITE:** One word is a kind of dance.

4. **BANANA BITE:** One word is something worn on a hand.

17

BANANA SHAKES

LEVEL

Each of the following six-letter sets can be rearranged to spell out a common word that starts with B E**,** E N **or** F L **and/or ends with** I C**,** T E **or** T H**. How quickly can you find all the words?**

A E O R T T

A B E R T Y

D E E N R U

C E H I N T

A C I M O S

E E G I N N

B C E E M O

E F L N T U

E G H L N T

A H M R T W

A F L O R V

E E F R T U

18

Each of the words below can be turned into another word on the list by changing one letter and then rearranging them all to form a new word. For example, REGIMENT can be turned into STEERING by changing the M to an S, so they would be a pair. How quickly can you find all the pairs?

Pairs

1. A R M A D A

2. P A Y O U T   ___ ___

3. P U L P I T   ___ ___

4. N A P K I N   ___ ___

5. P A R I T Y   ___ ___

6. M A R A U D   ___ ___

7. A R M P I T   ___ ___

8. R H U M B A

9. U P L I F T

10. U T O P I A

11. B A R I U M

12. U N L A I D

13. K I D N A P

14. A L U M N I

BANANA LEAVES

Using the 15 tiles in the bunch, fill in the spaces below according to the directions given.

LEVEL

Use the tiles in the bunch to make 24 different common four-letter words. Each word must include the letter U.

20

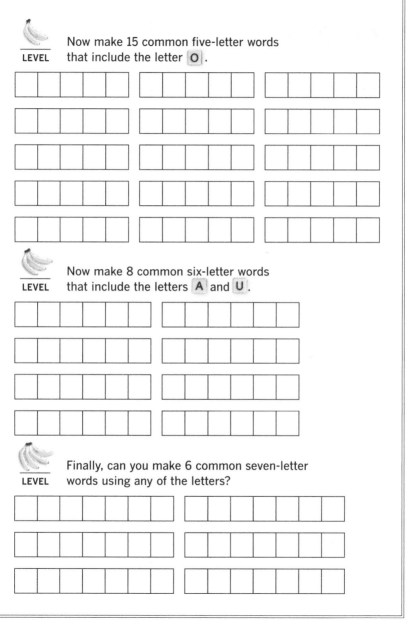

Now make 15 common five-letter words
that include the letter O.

Now make 8 common six-letter words
that include the letters A and U.

Finally, can you make 6 common seven-letter
words using any of the letters?

21

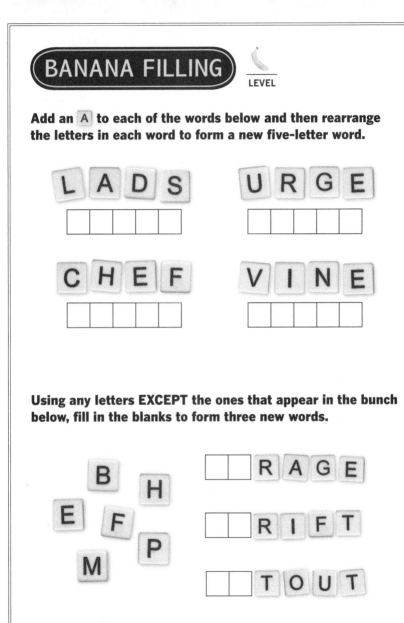

BANANA FILLING

LEVEL

Add an A to each of the words below and then rearrange the letters in each word to form a new five-letter word.

L A D S

⬜⬜⬜⬜⬜

U R G E

⬜⬜⬜⬜⬜

C H E F

⬜⬜⬜⬜⬜

V I N E

⬜⬜⬜⬜⬜

Using any letters EXCEPT the ones that appear in the bunch below, fill in the blanks to form three new words.

B H
E F
M P

⬜⬜ R A G E

⬜⬜ R I F T

⬜⬜ T O U T

22

Using three of the tiles from each bunch on the left, fill in the blanks on the right to make a six-letter word that connects the grid.

GO BANANAS!

LEVEL

Use all 21 tiles in this bunch to create a collection of connecting and intersecting common words in the grid below. The words may be horizontal or vertical, reading left to right or top to bottom.

You decide to dump a Q and draw a V, W and G. Add them to your bunch and rearrange the words and letters in your grid as needed to form a new collection of intersecting words.

LEVEL

For each of the word groups below, change one letter in the top word to one of the letters that appears in the bottom word, then rearrange the tiles as needed to form a new common word. Do the same with each new word until you arrive at the bottom word. For example, one path from **BARK** to **PLUM** is **BARK, MARK, RAMP, RUMP, PLUM.**

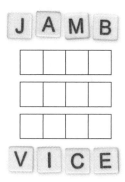

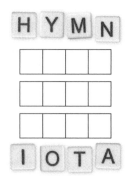

Each of the two-letter groups below may be extended both on the right and the left to form a six-letter word. Drawing from the tiles directly above each group, fill in the blanks to find the words as quickly as you can.

A C E L P W

☐ ☐ S H ☐ ☐

F H L M O Y

☐ ☐ A S ☐ ☐

A C E G H N

☐ ☐ M I ☐ ☐

C E E F L O

☐ ☐ M A ☐ ☐

C E M N T U

☐ ☐ R E ☐ ☐

BANANA SPLITS

For each of the three words below, change one letter to an N and then rearrange the letters to spell a chemical element.

O N C E

⬜⬜⬜⬜

B I T

⬜⬜⬜

C A R G O

⬜⬜⬜⬜⬜⬜

For each of the three words below, change one letter to an O and then rearrange the letters to spell a type of currency.

S T E P

⬜⬜⬜⬜

R U L E

⬜⬜⬜⬜

U P E N D

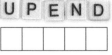

⬜⬜⬜⬜⬜⬜

Replace each of the question marks below with one of the vowels A, E, I, O or U and then rearrange the letters to form a common word. Each vowel will be used only once.

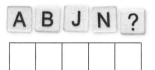

BANANA TREES

LEVEL

Use this bunch of 15 tiles to fill in each of the four grids below. To get you started, a few tiles from the bunch have been placed in each grid. Using the remaining tiles in the bunch, find words that complete each grid.

1.

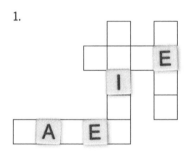

2.

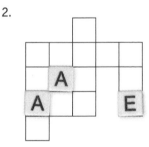

3.

4.

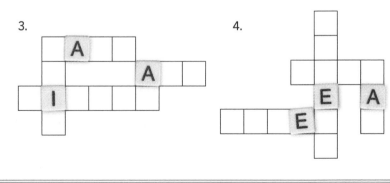

Use the 15 tiles in this bunch to create words that fit into the grids below. You will reuse this bunch for each of the four grids. The BANANA BITES provide hints to help you solve each grid.

LEVEL

1. **BANANA BITE:**
One word is a kind of bird.

2. **BANANA BITE:**
One word is a kind of portal.

3. **BANANA BITE:**
One word means "those who give."

4. **BANANA BITE:**
One word is something you smell.

BANANA SHAKES

LEVEL

Each of the following six-letter sets can be rearranged to spell out a common word that starts with S T, C H or I N and/or ends with N T, E D or O N. How quickly can you find all the words?

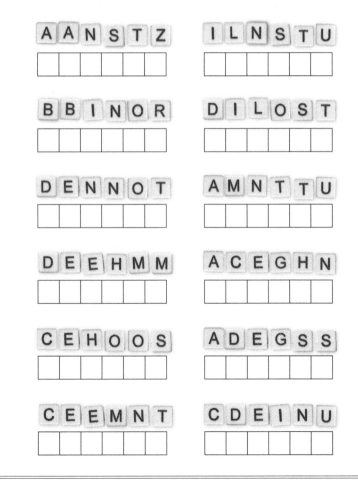

A A N S T Z

B B I N O R

D E N N O T

D E E H M M

C E H O O S

C E E M N T

I L N S T U

D I L O S T

A M N T T U

A C E G H N

A D E G S S

C D E I N U

Each of the words below can be turned into another word on the list by changing one letter and then rearranging them all to form a new word. For example, REGIMENT can be turned into STEERING by changing the M to an S, so they would be a pair. How quickly can you find all the pairs?

	Pairs
1. D I L U T E	___ ___
2. S E P T I C	___ ___
3. M U T A N T	___ ___
4. M A N U R E	___ ___
5. U R B A N E	___ ___
6. A U T U M N	___ ___
7. D E A C O N	
8. W I L T E D	
9. S E C O N D	
10. A U R O R A	
11. M I C R O N	
12. I N S E C T	
13. I N F O R M	
14. A R B O U R	

Using the 15 tiles in the bunch, fill in the spaces below according to the directions given.

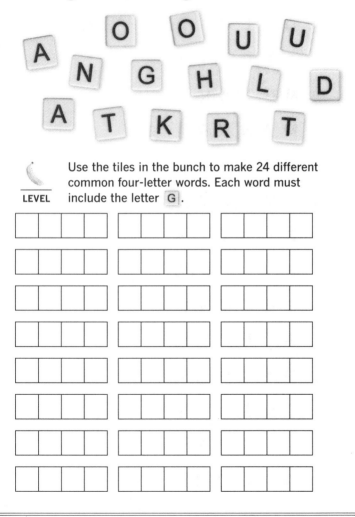

LEVEL

Use the tiles in the bunch to make 24 different common four-letter words. Each word must include the letter G.

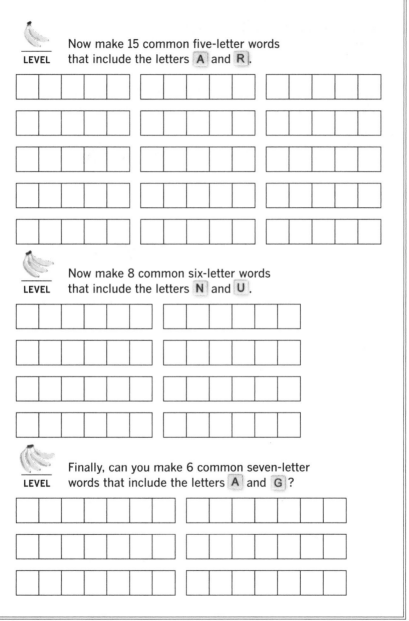

Now make 15 common five-letter words that include the letters **A** and **R**.

Now make 8 common six-letter words that include the letters **N** and **U**.

Finally, can you make 6 common seven-letter words that include the letters **A** and **G**?

BANANA FILLING

LEVEL

Add an ▪ **to each of the words below and then rearrange the letters in each word to form a new five-letter word.**

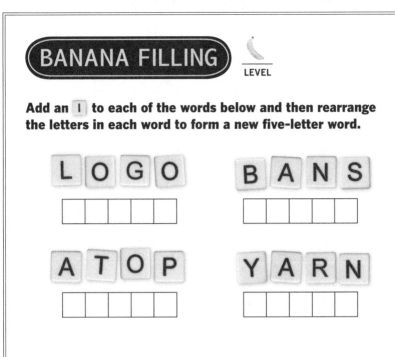

L O G O

☐☐☐☐☐

B A N S

☐☐☐☐☐

A T O P

☐☐☐☐☐

Y A R N

☐☐☐☐☐

Using any letters EXCEPT the ones that appear in the bunch below, fill in the blanks to form three new words.

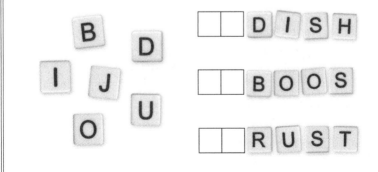

B D

I J

U

O

☐☐ D I S H

☐☐ B O O S

☐☐ R U S T

Using three of the tiles from each bunch on the left, fill in the blanks on the right to make a six-letter word that connects the grid.

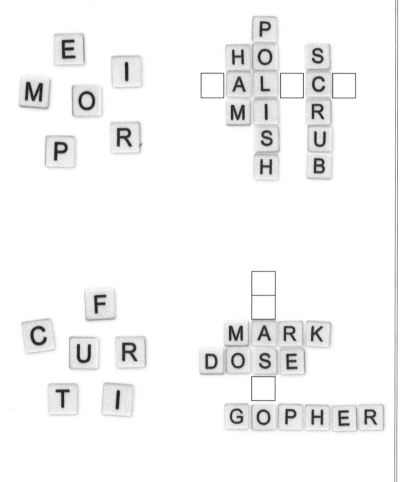

GO BANANAS!

LEVEL

Use all 21 tiles in this bunch to create a collection of connecting and intersecting common words in the grid below. The words may be horizontal or vertical, reading left to right or top to bottom.

Add an O to your bunch. Rearrange the words and letters in your grid as needed to form a new collection of intersecting words.

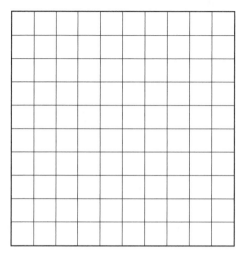

Now add a V !

LEVEL

For each of the word groups below, change one letter in the top word to one of the letters that appears in the bottom word, then rearrange the tiles as needed to form a new common word. Do the same with each new word until you arrive at the bottom word. For example, one path from **BARK** to **PLUM** is **BARK, MARK, RAMP, RUMP, PLUM**.

Each of the two-letter groups below may be extended both on the right and the left to form a six-letter word. Drawing from the tiles directly above each group, fill in the blanks to find the words as quickly as you can.

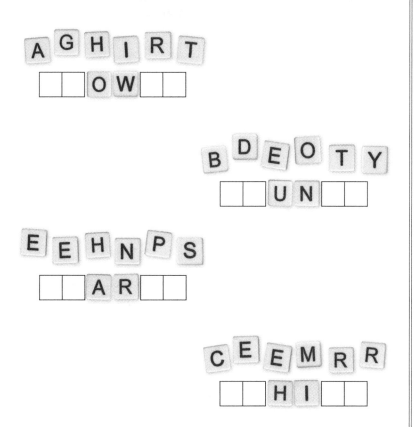

A G H I R T
☐ ☐ O W ☐ ☐

B D E O T Y
☐ ☐ U N ☐ ☐

E E H N P S
☐ ☐ A R ☐ ☐

C E E M R R
☐ ☐ H I ☐ ☐

M N O P R T
☐ ☐ I T ☐ ☐

BANANA SPLITS

LEVEL

For each of the three words below, change one letter to an E and then rearrange the letters to spell a part of the body.

HOLE

KEY

KINDLY

For each of the three words below, change one letter to an A and then rearrange the letters to spell a type of reptile.

PUS

NECKS

BRONC

Replace each of the question marks below with one of the vowels A , E , I , O or U and then rearrange the letters to form a common word. Each vowel will be used only once.

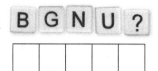

BANANA TREES

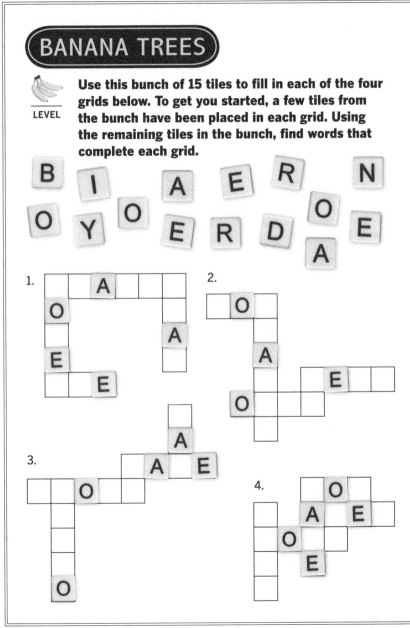

Use this bunch of 15 tiles to fill in each of the four grids below. To get you started, a few tiles from the bunch have been placed in each grid. Using the remaining tiles in the bunch, find words that complete each grid.

LEVEL

44

Use the 15 tiles in this bunch to create words that fit into the grids below. You will reuse this bunch for each of the four grids. The BANANA BITES provide hints to help you solve each grid.

1. **BANANA BITE:** One word is part of the body.

2. **BANANA BITE:** One word is a kind of soup.

3. **BANANA BITE:** One word is a part of the face.

4. **BANANA BITE:** One word is a season.

BANANA SHAKES

LEVEL

Each of the following six-letter sets can be rearranged to spell out a common word that starts with A B **,** D E **or** P R **and/or ends with** T Y **,** A L **or** N E **. How quickly can you find all the words?**

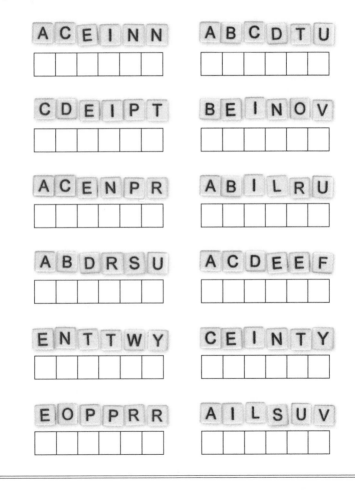

A C E I N N

A B C D T U

C D E I P T

B E I N O V

A C E N P R

A B I L R U

A B D R S U

A C D E E F

E N T T W Y

C E I N T Y

E O P P R R

A I L S U V

Each of the words below can be turned into another word on the list by changing one letter and then rearranging them all to form a new word. For example, REGIMENT can be turned into STEERING by changing the M to an S, so they would be a pair. How quickly can you find all the pairs?

Pairs

1. I M P A L E

2. R E S A Y S

3. D E N O T E

4. B R U I S E

5. M A L I C E

6. C U R A T E

7. P H O T O N

8. S U P E R B

9. A S S U R E

10. C O M B E D

11. F A U C E T

12. B O D I C E

13. O P T I O N

14. O P E N E D

____ ____

____ ____

____ ____

____ ____

____ ____

____ ____

BANANA LEAVES

Using the 15 tiles in the bunch, fill in the spaces below according to the directions given.

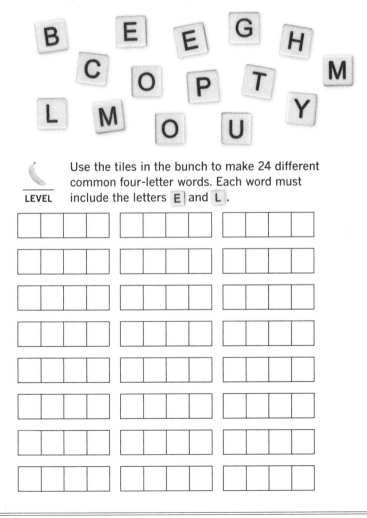

Use the tiles in the bunch to make 24 different common four-letter words. Each word must include the letters E and L.

LEVEL

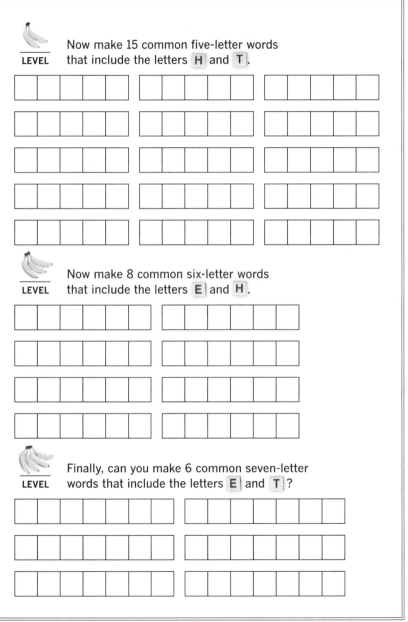

LEVEL Now make 15 common five-letter words that include the letters **H** and **T**.

LEVEL Now make 8 common six-letter words that include the letters **E** and **H**.

LEVEL Finally, can you make 6 common seven-letter words that include the letters **E** and **T**?

Add a U **to each of the words below and then rearrange the letters in each word to form a new five-letter word.**

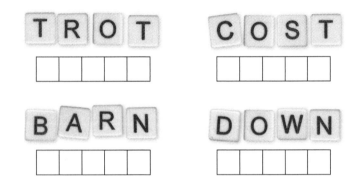

T R O T

C O S T

B A R N

D O W N

Using any letters EXCEPT the ones that appear in the bunch below, fill in the blanks to form three new words.

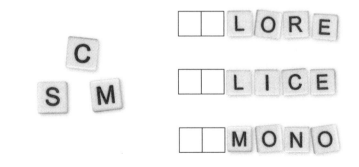

C
S   M

L O R E

L I C E

M O N O

Using three of the tiles from each bunch on the left, fill in the blanks on the right to make a six-letter word that connects the grid.

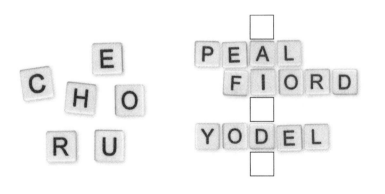

GO BANANAS!

LEVEL

Use all 21 tiles in this bunch to create a collection of connecting and intersecting common words in the grid below. The words may be horizontal or vertical, reading left to right or top to bottom.

You decide to dump an X and draw an N, D and I. Add them to your bunch and rearrange the words and letters in your grid as needed to form a new collection of intersecting words.

BANANA BOATS

LEVEL

For each of the word groups below, change one letter in the top word to one of the letters that appears in the bottom word, then rearrange the tiles as needed to form a new common word. Do the same with each new word until you arrive at the bottom word. For example, one path from BARK to PLUM is BARK, MARK, RAMP, RUMP, PLUM.

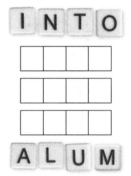

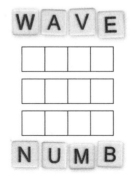

Each of the two-letter groups below may be extended both on the right and the left to form a six-letter word. Drawing from the tiles directly above each group, fill in the blanks to find the words as quickly as you can.

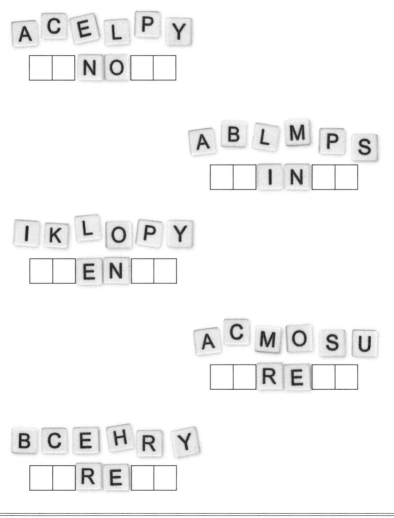

A C E L P Y

☐ ☐ N O ☐ ☐

A B L M P S

☐ ☐ I N ☐ ☐

I K L O P Y

☐ ☐ E N ☐ ☐

A C M O S U

☐ ☐ R E ☐ ☐

B C E H R Y

☐ R E ☐ ☐

BANANA SPLITS

LEVEL

For each of the three words below, change one letter to a Y **and then rearrange the letters to spell a word related to the weather.**

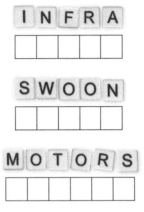

I N F R A

☐ ☐ ☐ ☐ ☐

S W O O N

☐ ☐ ☐ ☐ ☐

M O T O R S

☐ ☐ ☐ ☐ ☐ ☐

For each of the three words below, change one letter to an O **and then rearrange the letters to spell a word related to music.**

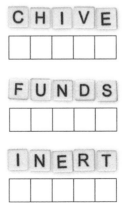

C H I V E

☐ ☐ ☐ ☐ ☐

F U N D S

☐ ☐ ☐ ☐ ☐

I N E R T

☐ ☐ ☐ ☐ ☐

Replace each of the question marks below with one of the vowels A, E, I, O or U and then rearrange the letters to form a common word. Each vowel will be used only once.

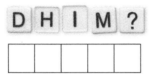

BANANA TREES

LEVEL

Use this bunch of 15 tiles to fill in each of the four grids below. To get you started, a few tiles from the bunch have been placed in each grid. Using the remaining tiles in the bunch, find words that complete each grid.

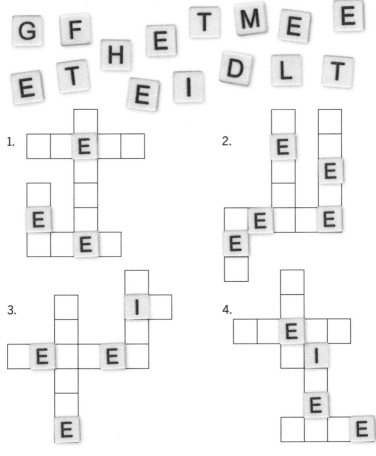

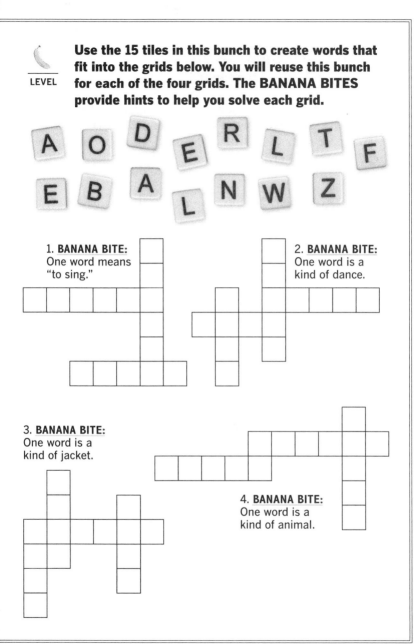

Use the 15 tiles in this bunch to create words that fit into the grids below. You will reuse this bunch for each of the four grids. The BANANA BITES provide hints to help you solve each grid.

LEVEL

A O D E R L T F
E B A L N W Z

1. **BANANA BITE:** One word means "to sing."

2. **BANANA BITE:** One word is a kind of dance.

3. **BANANA BITE:** One word is a kind of jacket.

4. **BANANA BITE:** One word is a kind of animal.

Each of the following six-letter sets can be rearranged to spell out a common word that starts with C O, M I or T H and/or ends with A N, E R or A Y. How quickly can you find all the words?

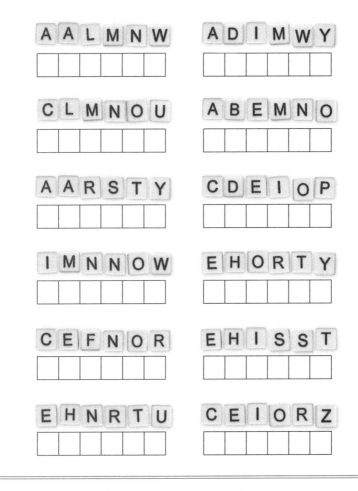

A A L M N W

A D I M W Y

C L M N O U

A B E M N O

A A R S T Y

C D E I O P

I M N N O W

E H O R T Y

C E F N O R

E H I S S T

E H N R T U

C E I O R Z

60

Each of the words below can be turned into another word on the list by changing one letter and then rearranging them all to form a new word. For example, REGIMENT can be turned into STEERING by changing the M to an S, so they would be a pair. How quickly can you find all the pairs?

1. D I V I N E

2. E N R A G E

3. M O L T E N

4. A D R O I T

5. C L U M S Y

6. P O E T R Y

7. I N S I D E

8. P O R T E R

9. M U S C L E

10. E L V I S H

11. T O R O I D

12. A G R E E D

13. L E M O N Y

14. S L E I G H

Pairs

___ ___

___ ___

─── ──

─── ──

─── ──

─── ──

Using the 15 tiles in the bunch, fill in the spaces below according to the directions given.

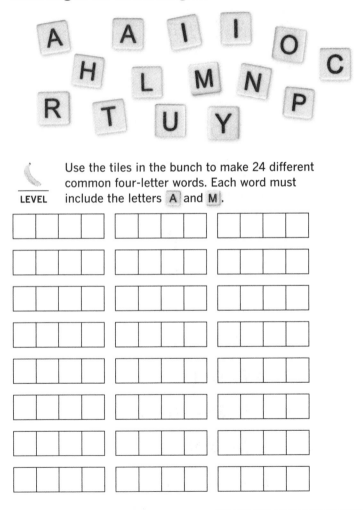

LEVEL

Use the tiles in the bunch to make 24 different common four-letter words. Each word must include the letters A and M.

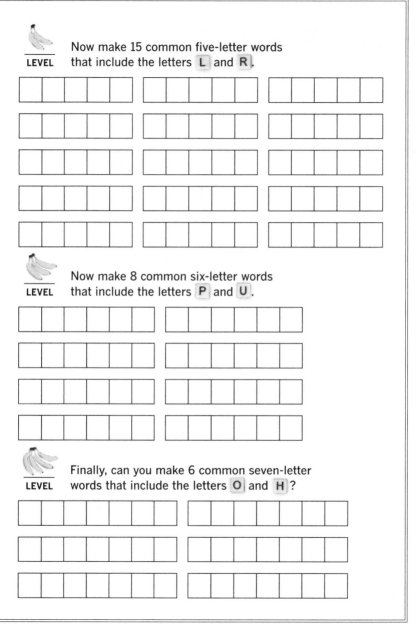

LEVEL Now make 15 common five-letter words that include the letters **L** and **R**.

LEVEL Now make 8 common six-letter words that include the letters **P** and **U**.

LEVEL Finally, can you make 6 common seven-letter words that include the letters **O** and **H**?

Add an E **to each of the words below and then rearrange the letters in each word to form a new five-letter word.**

Using any letters EXCEPT the ones that appear in the bunch below, fill in the blanks to form three new words.

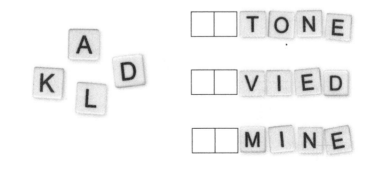

Using three of the tiles from each bunch on the left, fill in the blanks on the right to make a six-letter word that connects the grid.

GO BANANAS!

LEVEL

Use all 21 tiles in this bunch to create a collection of connecting and intersecting common words in the grid below. The words may be horizontal or vertical, reading left to right or top to bottom.

Add a G to your bunch. Rearrange the words and letters in your grid as needed to form a new collection of intersecting words.

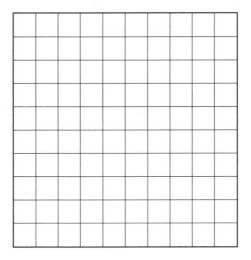

Now add a W !

LEVEL

For each of the word groups below, change one letter in the top word to one of the letters that appears in the bottom word, then rearrange the tiles as needed to form a new common word. Do the same with each new word until you arrive at the bottom word. For example, one path from **BARK to PLUM is BARK, MARK, RAMP, RUMP, PLUM.**

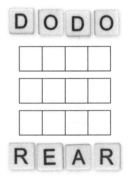

Each of the two-letter groups below may be extended both on the right and the left to form a six-letter word. Drawing from the tiles directly above each group, fill in the blanks to find the words as quickly as you can.

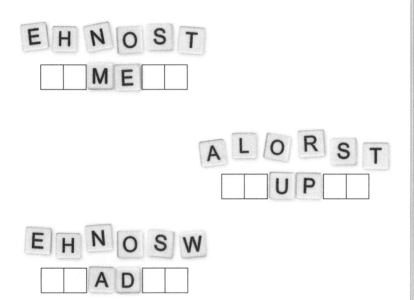

E H N O S T

☐ ☐ M E ☐ ☐

A L O R S T

☐ ☐ U P ☐ ☐

E H N O S W

☐ ☐ A D ☐ ☐

E L P S U Y

☐ ☐ E F ☐ ☐

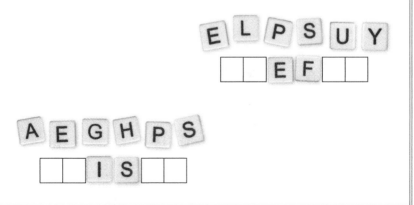

A E G H P S

☐ ☐ I S ☐ ☐

For each of the three words below, change one letter to a P and then rearrange the letters to spell a type of fruit or vegetable.

MULE

☐☐☐☐

LICKED

☐☐☐☐☐☐

PLACE

☐☐☐☐☐

For each of the three words below, change one letter to a T and then rearrange the letters to spell a part of the body.

PHOTO

☐☐☐☐☐

HOKUM

☐☐☐☐☐

REACH

☐☐☐☐☐

Replace each of the question marks below with one of the vowels A, E, I, O **or** U **and then rearrange the letters to form a common word. Each vowel will be used only once.**

BANANA TREES

Use this bunch of 15 tiles to fill in each of the four grids below. To get you started, a few tiles from the bunch have been placed in each grid. Using the remaining tiles in the bunch, find words that complete each grid.

LEVEL

1.

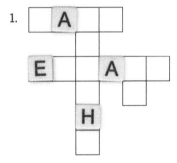

2.

3.

4.

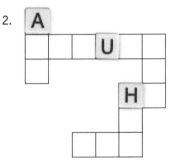

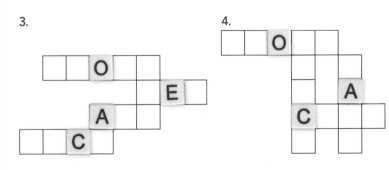

72

LEVEL

Use the 15 tiles in this bunch to create words that fit into the grids below. You will reuse this bunch for each of the four grids. The BANANA BITES provide hints to help you solve each grid.

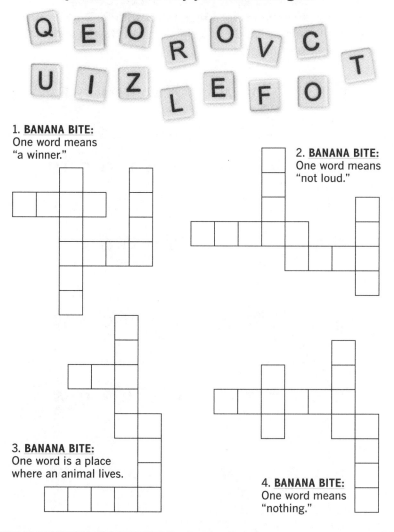

Q E O R O V C T
U I Z L E F O

1. BANANA BITE:
One word means "a winner."

2. BANANA BITE:
One word means "not loud."

3. BANANA BITE:
One word is a place where an animal lives.

4. BANANA BITE:
One word means "nothing."

BANANA SHAKES

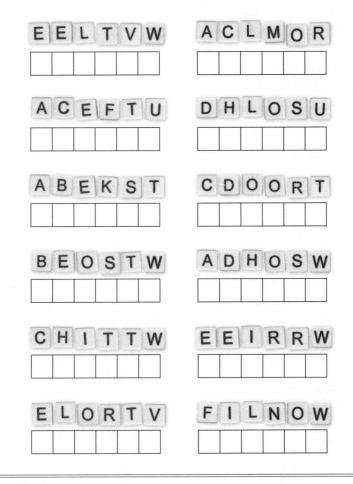

LEVEL

Each of the following six-letter sets can be rearranged to spell out a common word that starts with R E, S H or T W and/or ends with E T, O R or O W. How quickly can you find all the words?

E E L T V W

A C L M O R

A C E F T U

D H L O S U

A B E K S T

C D O O R T

B E O S T W

A D H O S W

C H I T T W

E E I R R W

E L O R T V

F I L N O W

Each of the words below can be turned into another word on the list by changing one letter and then rearranging them all to form a new word. For example, REGIMENT can be turned into STEERING by changing the M to an S, so they would be a pair. How quickly can you find all the pairs?

Pairs

1. WILLED
2. MISFIT
3. LANDER
4. SIENNA
5. ARTIST
6. LILIED
7. NEARLY
8. SEWAGE
9. ISTHMI
10. GUINEA
11. GEEGAW
12. ENSIGN
13. THIRST
14. ENIGMA

___ ___
___ ___
___ ___
___ ___
___ ___
___ ___
___ ___

BANANA LEAVES

Using the 15 tiles in the bunch, fill in the spaces below according to the directions given.

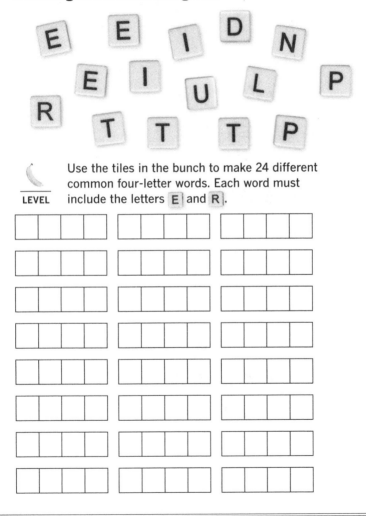

LEVEL

Use the tiles in the bunch to make 24 different common four-letter words. Each word must include the letters E and R.

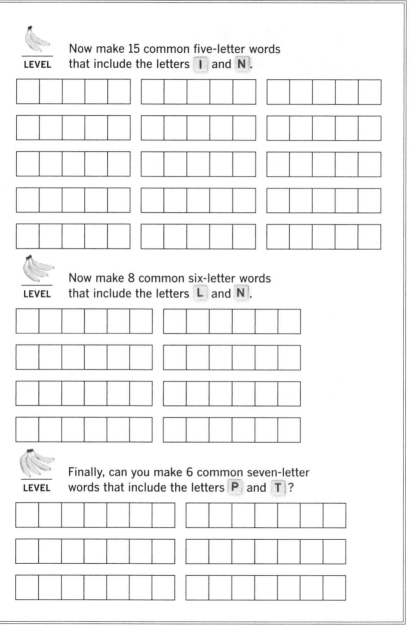

Now make 15 common five-letter words that include the letters **I** and **N**.

Now make 8 common six-letter words that include the letters **L** and **N**.

Finally, can you make 6 common seven-letter words that include the letters **P** and **T**?

Add an O to each of the words below and then rearrange the letters in each word to form a new five-letter word.

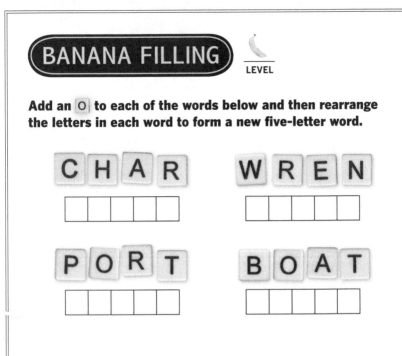

C H A R

W R E N

P O R T

B O A T

Using any letters EXCEPT the ones that appear in the bunch below, fill in the blanks to form three new words.

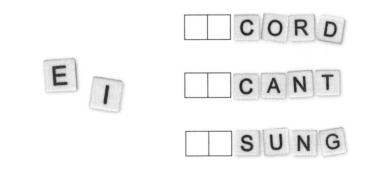

E   I

_ _ C O R D

_ _ C A N T

_ _ S U N G

Using three of the tiles from each bunch on the left, fill in the blanks on the right to make a six-letter word that connects the grid.

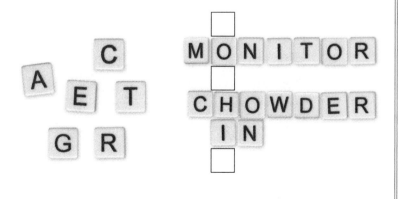

Use all **21 tiles** in this bunch to create a collection of connecting and intersecting common words in the grid below. The words may be horizontal or vertical, reading left to right or top to bottom.

You decide to dump a K and draw an A, M and O. Add them to your bunch and rearrange the words and letters in your grid as needed to form a new collection of intersecting words.

For each of the word groups below, change one letter in the top word to one of the letters that appears in the bottom word, then rearrange the tiles as needed to form a new common word. Do the same with each new word until you arrive at the bottom word. For example, one path from BARK to PLUM is BARK, MARK, RAMP, RUMP, PLUM.

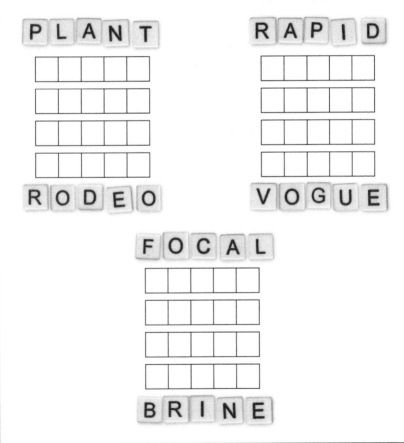

P L A N T

R O D E O

R A P I D

V O G U E

F O C A L

B R I N E

Each of the three-letter groups below may be extended both on the right and the left to form a seven-letter word. Drawing from the tiles directly above each group, fill in the blanks to find the words as quickly as you can.

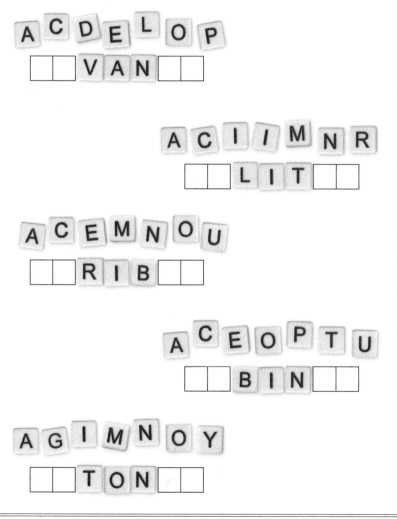

A C D E L O P

☐ ☐ V A N ☐ ☐

A C I I M N R

☐ ☐ L I T ☐ ☐

A C E M N O U

☐ ☐ R I B ☐ ☐

A C E O P T U

☐ ☐ B I N ☐ ☐

A G I M N O Y

☐ ☐ T O N ☐ ☐

For each of the three words below, change one letter to a U and then rearrange the letters to spell a word related to basketball.

G O L F

⬜⬜⬜⬜

A P T L Y

⬜⬜⬜⬜⬜

G R A D E

⬜⬜⬜⬜⬜

For each of the three words below, change one letter to an N and then rearrange the letters to spell a type of animal.

A D A P T

⬜⬜⬜⬜⬜

C H I E F

⬜⬜⬜⬜⬜

H E A V Y

⬜⬜⬜⬜⬜

Replace each of the question marks below with one of the vowels A, E, I, O or U and then rearrange the letters to form a common word. Each vowel will be used only once.

BANANA TREES

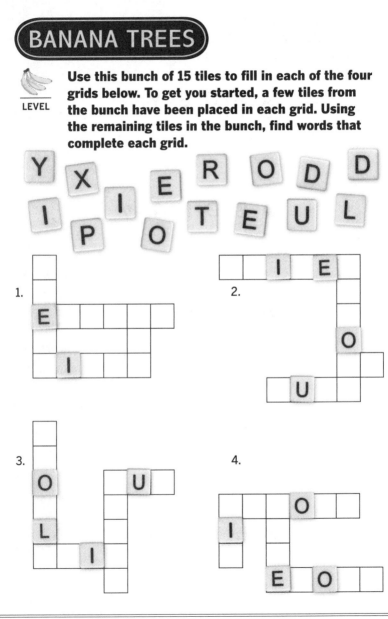

LEVEL

Use this bunch of 15 tiles to fill in each of the four grids below. To get you started, a few tiles from the bunch have been placed in each grid. Using the remaining tiles in the bunch, find words that complete each grid.

Y X I E R O D D
I P I O T E U L

1.

E

I

2.

I E

O

U

3.

O

L I

U

4.

I O

E O

Use the 15 tiles in this bunch to create words that fit into the grids below. You will reuse this bunch for each of the four grids. The BANANA BITES provide hints to help you solve each grid.

LEVEL

A I D H G A V T
E M A E N D E T

1. **BANANA BITE:**
One word means "more than once."

2. **BANANA BITE:**
One word is a person who cleans.

3. **BANANA BITE:**
One word means "angry."

4. **BANANA BITE:**
One word means "a place of safety."

BANANA SHAKES

LEVEL

Each of the following seven-letter sets can be rearranged to spell out a common word that starts with INS, RET **or** UNS **and/or ends with** IER, ANT **or** OUS. **How quickly can you find all the words?**

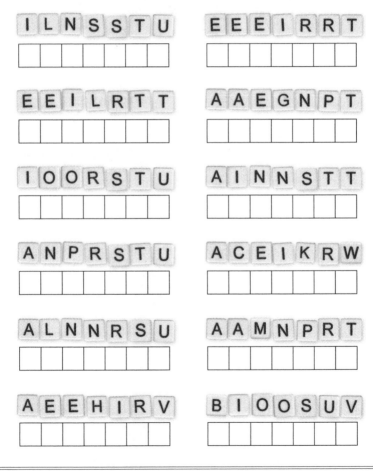

ILNSSTU

EEEIRRT

EEILRTT

AAEGNPT

IOORSTU

AINNSTT

ANPRSTU

ACEIKRW

ALNNRSU

AAMNPRT

AEEHIRV

BIOOSUV

Each of the words below can be turned into another word on the list by changing one letter and then rearranging them all to form a new word. For example, REGIMENT can be turned into STEERING by changing the M to an S, so they would be a pair. How quickly can you find all the pairs?

1. E N F O R C E

2. R U N A W A Y

3. I N T E N S E

4. C O M B I N E

5. H E F T I N G

6. C O N F E R S

7. A C O L Y T E

8. U N A W A R E

9. P I V O T A L

10. S I X T E E N

11. F I G H T E R

12. T O P I C A L

13. C O L L A T E

14. B E N Z O I C

Pairs

___ ___

___ ___

___ ___

___ ___

___ ___

___ ___

___ ___

BANANA LEAVES

Using the 15 tiles in the bunch, fill in the spaces below according to the directions given.

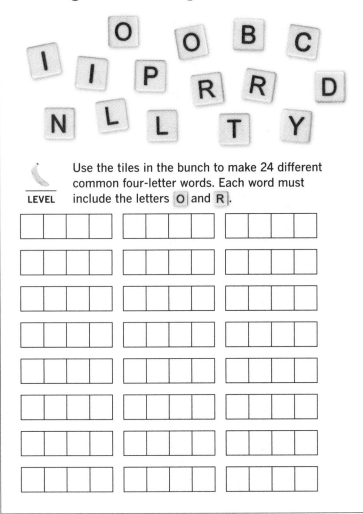

LEVEL

Use the tiles in the bunch to make 24 different common four-letter words. Each word must include the letters O and R.

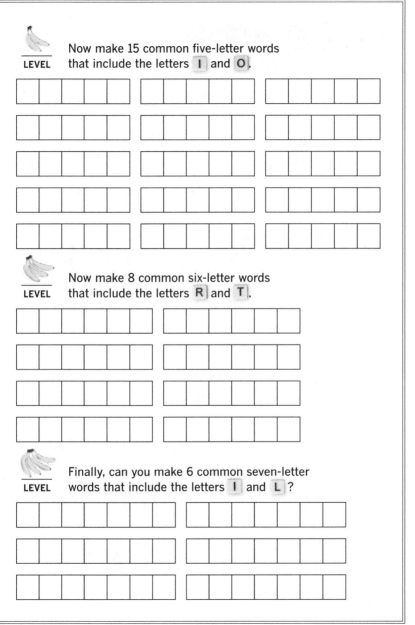

Now make 15 common five-letter words
that include the letters **I** and **O**.

Now make 8 common six-letter words
that include the letters **R** and **T**.

Finally, can you make 6 common seven-letter
words that include the letters **I** and **L**?

LEVEL

LEVEL

LEVEL

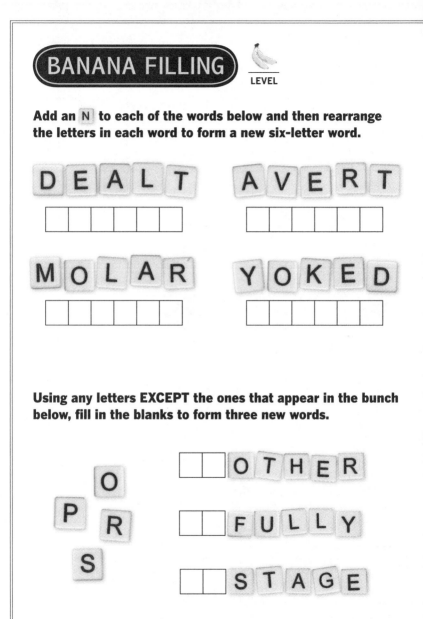

BANANA FILLING

LEVEL

Add an N to each of the words below and then rearrange the letters in each word to form a new six-letter word.

DEALT

⬜⬜⬜⬜⬜⬜

AVERT

⬜⬜⬜⬜⬜⬜

MOLAR

⬜⬜⬜⬜⬜⬜

YOKED

⬜⬜⬜⬜⬜⬜

Using any letters EXCEPT the ones that appear in the bunch below, fill in the blanks to form three new words.

P O R S

⬜⬜ OTHER

⬜⬜ FULLY

⬜⬜ STAGE

Using four of the tiles from each bunch on the left, fill in the blanks on the right to make a seven-letter word that connects the grid.

GO BANANAS!

LEVEL

Use all 21 tiles in this bunch to create a collection of connecting and intersecting common words in the grid below. The words may be horizontal or vertical, reading left to right or top to bottom.

Add a V to your bunch. Rearrange the words and letters in your grid as needed to form a new collection of intersecting words.

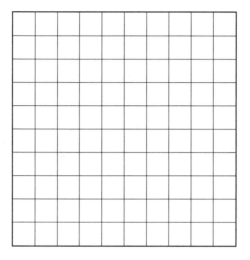

Now add an X!

BANANA BOATS

LEVEL

For each of the word groups below, change one letter in the top word to one of the letters that appears in the bottom word, then rearrange the tiles as needed to form a new common word. Do the same with each new word until you arrive at the bottom word. For example, one path from BARK to PLUM is BARK, MARK, RAMP, RUMP, PLUM.

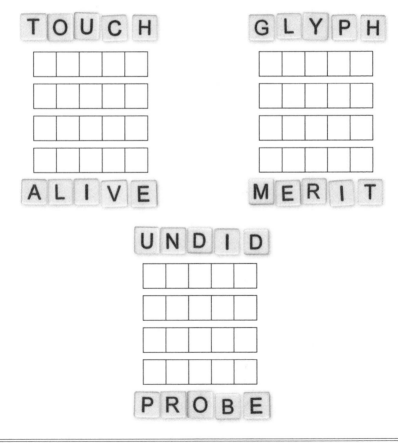

Each of the three-letter groups below may be extended both on the right and the left to form a seven-letter word. Drawing from the tiles directly above each group, fill in the blanks to find the words as quickly as you can.

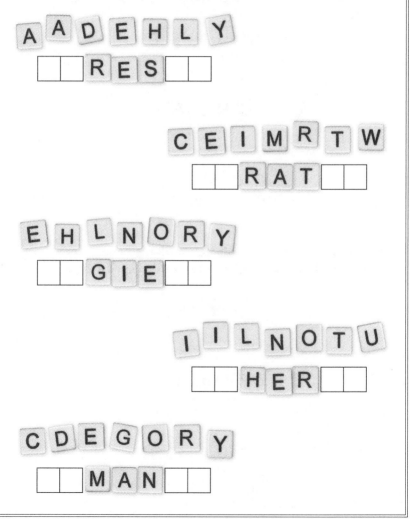

A A D E H L Y
☐ ☐ R E S ☐ ☐

C E I M R T W
☐ ☐ R A T ☐ ☐

E H L N O R Y
☐ ☐ G I E ☐ ☐

I I L N O T U
☐ ☐ H E R ☐ ☐

C D E G O R Y
☐ ☐ M A N ☐ ☐

BANANA SPLITS

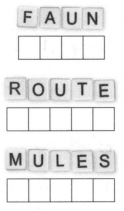

LEVEL

For each of the three words below, change one letter to an N and then rearrange the letters to spell a type of food.

R U P E E

⬚ ⬚ ⬚ ⬚ ⬚

C H E A P

⬚ ⬚ ⬚ ⬚ ⬚

O U T L A W

⬚ ⬚ ⬚ ⬚ ⬚ ⬚

For each of the three words below, change one letter to a T and then rearrange the letters to spell a type of fish.

F A U N

⬚ ⬚ ⬚ ⬚

R O U T E

⬚ ⬚ ⬚ ⬚ ⬚

M U L E S

⬚ ⬚ ⬚ ⬚ ⬚

Replace each of the question marks below with one of the vowels A, E, I, O or U and then rearrange the letters to form a common word. Each vowel will be used only once.

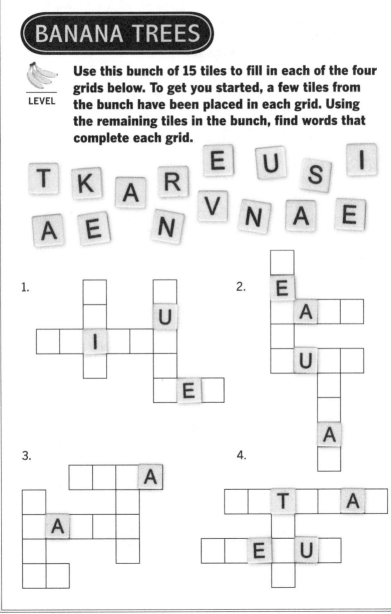

BANANA TREES

Use this bunch of 15 tiles to fill in each of the four grids below. To get you started, a few tiles from the bunch have been placed in each grid. Using the remaining tiles in the bunch, find words that complete each grid.

LEVEL

T K A R E U S I
A E N V N A E

1.

2.

3.

4.

LEVEL

Use the 15 tiles in this bunch to create words that fit into the grids below. You will reuse this bunch for each of the four grids. The BANANA BITES provide hints to help you solve each grid.

1. BANANA BITE:
One word is something you put in a drink.

2. BANANA BITE:
One word means "a heroic achievement."

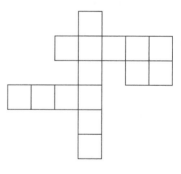

3. BANANA BITE:
One word is part of an animal.

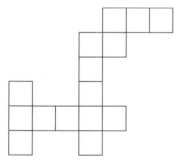

4. BANANA BITE:
One word means "head honcho."

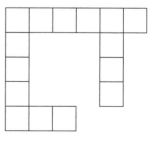

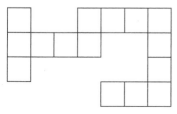

BANANA SHAKES

LEVEL

Each of the following seven-letter sets can be rearranged to spell out a common word that starts with TRI**,** SUB **or** COM **and/or ends with** ER**,** FUL **or** GHT**. How quickly can you find all the words?**

D G H O R T U

G H I P T T U

C E E M O P T

A B F H L S U

A I I L R T V

A B D E H S U

E E F R R S U

I I N R T T Y

A C E O R R S

E E F G L L U

C D E M M N O

B D E I S S U

Each of the words below can be turned into another word on the list by changing one letter and then rearranging them all to form a new word. For example, REGIMENT can be turned into STEERING by changing the M to an S, so they would be a pair. How quickly can you find all the pairs?

1. V I R T U A L   Pairs
2. R U N D O W N   —— ——
3. Y A M M E R S   —— ——
4. O R I G A M I   —— ——
5. R I V U L E T   —— ——
6. N O T C H E D   —— ——
7. R O A M I N G   —— ——
8. T O E N A I L
9. U N O W N E D
10. R E F U S A L
11. S U M M A R Y
12. F U N E R A L
13. V I O L A T E
14. D O Z E N T H

BANANA LEAVES

Using the 15 tiles in the bunch, fill in the spaces below according to the directions given.

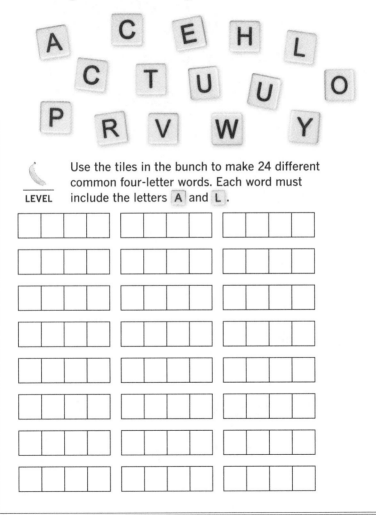

Use the tiles in the bunch to make 24 different common four-letter words. Each word must include the letters A and L.

LEVEL

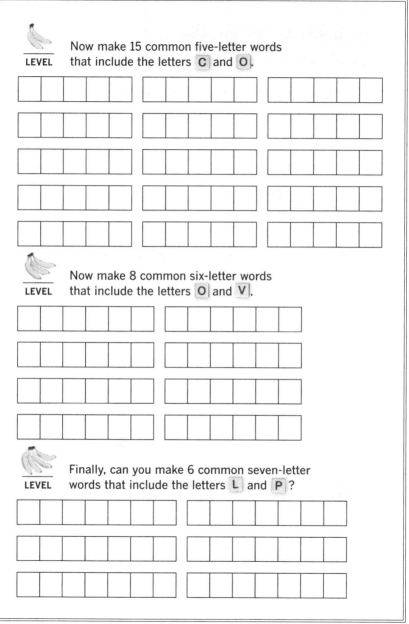

Now make 15 common five-letter words that include the letters **C** and **O**.

LEVEL

Now make 8 common six-letter words that include the letters **O** and **V**.

LEVEL

Finally, can you make 6 common seven-letter words that include the letters **L** and **P**?

LEVEL

BANANA FILLING

Add an A to each of the words below and then rearrange the letters in each word to form a new six-letter word.

BLURT

☐☐☐☐☐☐

CROWD

☐☐☐☐☐☐

COLIC

☐☐☐☐☐☐

CELLO

☐☐☐☐☐☐

Using any letters EXCEPT the ones that appear in the bunch below, fill in the blanks to form three new words.

S E

☐☐ READS

☐☐ DIALS

☐☐ AGUES

Using four of the tiles from each bunch on the left, fill in the blanks on the right to make a seven-letter word that connects the grid.

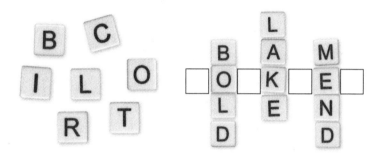

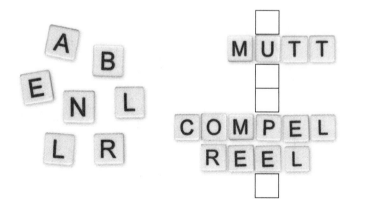

GO BANANAS!

LEVEL

Use all 21 tiles in this bunch to create a collection of connecting and intersecting common words in the grid below. The words may be horizontal or vertical, reading left to right or top to bottom.

You decide to dump a U and draw an O, O and O. Add them to your bunch and rearrange the words and letters in your grid as needed to form a new collection of intersecting words.

BANANA BOATS

LEVEL

For each of the word groups below, change one letter in the top word to one of the letters that appears in the bottom word, then rearrange the tiles as needed to form a new common word. Do the same with each new word until you arrive at the bottom word. For example, one path from BARK to PLUM is BARK, MARK, RAMP, RUMP, PLUM.

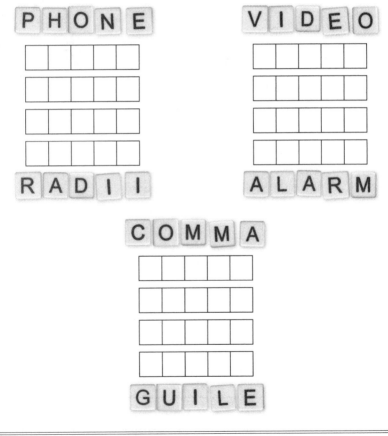

PHONE

RADII

VIDEO

ALARM

COMMA

GUILE

Each of the three-letter groups below may be extended
both on the right and the left to form a seven-letter word.
Drawing from the tiles directly above each group, fill in
the blanks to find the words as quickly as you can.

C D E I O T W

☐ ☐ A L E ☐ ☐

E G H M N O T

☐ ☐ B A R ☐ ☐

A G H R T U Y

☐ ☐ L I B ☐ ☐

A C E J L O R

☐ ☐ U R N ☐ ☐

A E E N R T V

☐ ☐ L I E ☐ ☐

LEVEL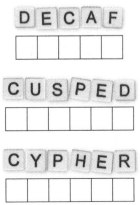

For each of the three words below, change one letter to an I **and then rearrange the letters to spell a type of musical instrument.**

L O V I N G

☐ ☐ ☐ ☐ ☐ ☐

A P R O N

☐ ☐ ☐ ☐ ☐

R A G O U T

☐ ☐ ☐ ☐ ☐ ☐

For each of the three words below, change one letter to an R **and then rearrange the letters to spell a type of tree.**

D E C A F

☐ ☐ ☐ ☐ ☐

C U S P E D

☐ ☐ ☐ ☐ ☐ ☐

C Y P H E R

☐ ☐ ☐ ☐ ☐ ☐

Replace each of the question marks below with one of the vowels A, E, I, O or U and then rearrange the letters to form a common word. Each vowel will be used only once.

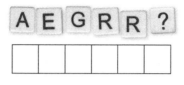

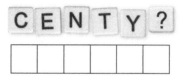

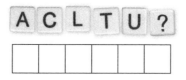

BANANA TREES

Use this bunch of 15 tiles to fill in each of the four grids below. To get you started, a few tiles from the bunch have been placed in each grid. Using the remaining tiles in the bunch, find words that complete each grid.

LEVEL

LEVEL

Use the 15 tiles in this bunch to create words that fit into the grids below. You will reuse this bunch for each of the four grids. The BANANA BITES provide hints to help you solve each grid.

1. **BANANA BITE:**
One word is a kind of drink.

2. **BANANA BITE:**
One word is a time of day.

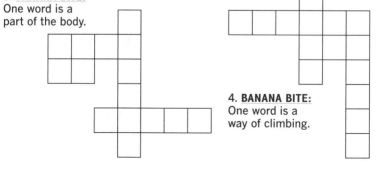

3. **BANANA BITE:**
One word is a part of the body.

4. **BANANA BITE:**
One word is a way of climbing.

BANANA SHAKES

LEVEL

Each of the following seven-letter sets can be rearranged to spell out a common word that starts with E M B , R E T or H E A D and/or ends with M A N , U R E or E S T . How quickly can you find all the words?

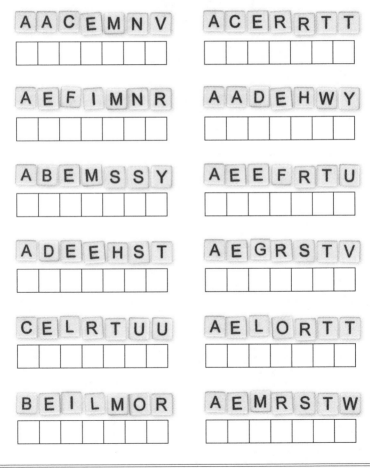

A A C E M N V

A C E R R T T

A E F I M N R

A A D E H W Y

A B E M S S Y

A E E F R T U

A D E E H S T

A E G R S T V

C E L R T U U

A E L O R T T

B E I L M O R

A E M R S T W

Each of the words below can be turned into another word on the list by changing one letter and then rearranging them all to form a new word. For example, REGIMENT can be turned into STEERING by changing the M to an S, so they would be a pair. How quickly can you find all the pairs?

Pairs

1. T O E L I K E
2. O U T L E A P
3. O U T W I N D
4. P O L L U T E
5. G O U L A S H
6. E M P T I L Y
7. A M E N I T Y
8. R E N E W A L
9. P E T I O L E
10. M I D T O W N
11. E N L A R G E
12. I N E P T L Y
13. T E A M I N G
14. P L O U G H S

___ ___
___ ___
___ ___
___ ___
___ ___
___ ___

BANANA LEAVES

Using the 15 tiles in the bunch, fill in the spaces below according to the directions given.

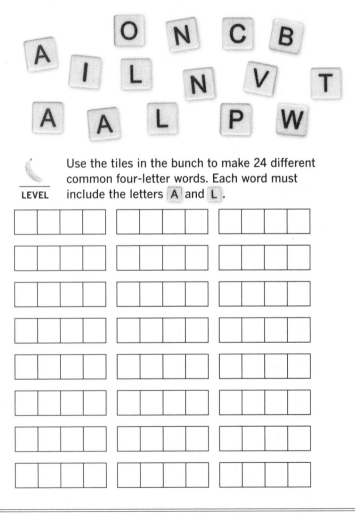

LEVEL

Use the tiles in the bunch to make 24 different common four-letter words. Each word must include the letters A and L.

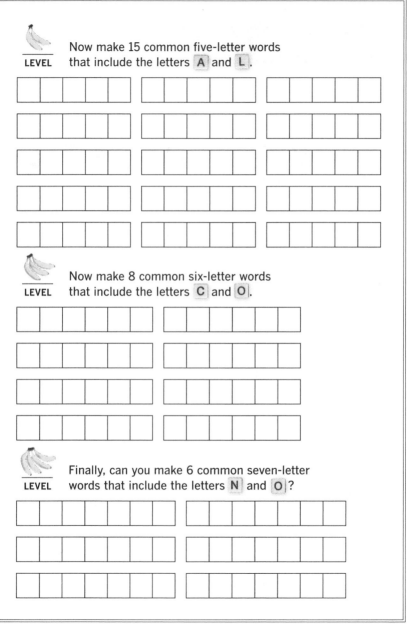

Now make 15 common five-letter words that include the letters **A** and **L**.

Now make 8 common six-letter words that include the letters **C** and **O**.

Finally, can you make 6 common seven-letter words that include the letters **N** and **O**?

BANANA FILLING

LEVEL

Add a D to each of the words below and then rearrange the letters in each word to form a new six-letter word.

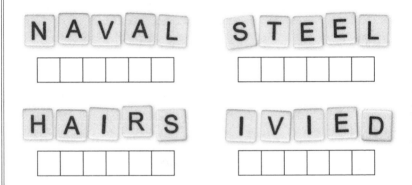

NAVAL

STEEL

HAIRS

IVIED

Using any letters EXCEPT the ones that appear in the bunch below, fill in the blanks to form three new words.

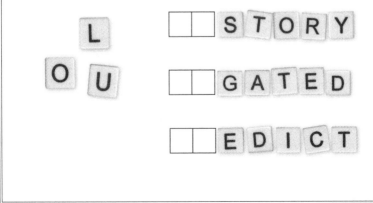

L

O U

☐☐ STORY

☐☐ GATED

☐☐ EDICT

120

Using four of the tiles from each bunch on the left, fill in the blanks on the right to make a seven-letter word that connects the grid.

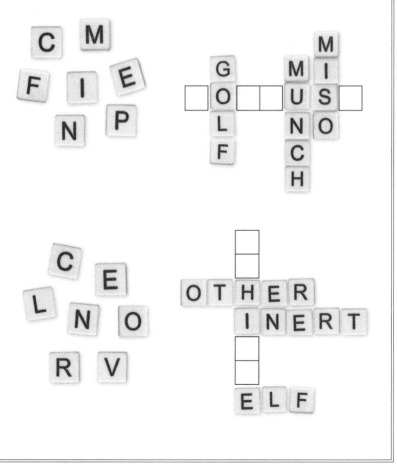

LEVEL

Use all 21 tiles in this bunch to create a collection of connecting and intersecting common words in the grid below. The words may be horizontal or vertical, reading left to right or top to bottom.

Add a **B** to your bunch. Rearrange the words and letters in your grid as needed to form a new collection of intersecting words.

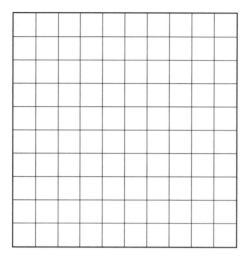

Now add an **R**!

LEVEL

For each of the word groups below, change one letter in the top word to one of the letters that appears in the bottom word, then rearrange the tiles as needed to form a new common word. Do the same with each new word until you arrive at the bottom word. For example, one path from **BARK** to **PLUM** is **BARK, MARK, RAMP, RUMP, PLUM.**

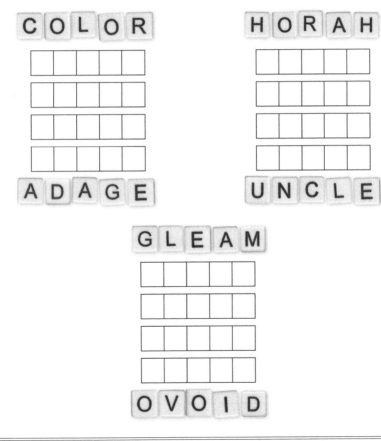

C O L O R

A D A G E

H O R A H

U N C L E

G L E A M

O V O I D

Each of the three-letter groups below may be extended both on the right and the left to form a seven-letter word. Drawing from the tiles directly above each group, fill in the blanks to find the words as quickly as you can.

C C H I L R U
[ ][ ] Y O N [ ][ ]

B D E I N O R
[ ][ ] S P A [ ][ ]

A A C G I L U
[ ][ ] M A N [ ][ ]

A E M O P R Y
[ ][ ] T A D [ ][ ]

A A H I R T U
[ ][ ] B I T [ ][ ]

LEVEL

For each of the three words below, change one letter to an R **and then rearrange the letters to spell a type of food.**

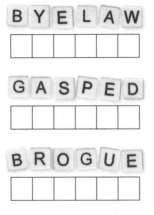

B Y E L A W

☐☐☐☐☐☐

G A S P E D

☐☐☐☐☐☐

B R O G U E

☐☐☐☐☐☐

For each of the three words below, change one letter to an O **and then rearrange the letters to spell a type of bird.**

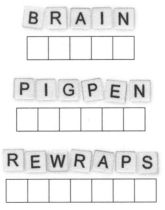

B R A I N

☐☐☐☐☐

P I G P E N

☐☐☐☐☐☐

R E W R A P S

☐☐☐☐☐☐☐

Replace each of the question marks below with one of the vowels A, E, I, O **or** U **and then rearrange the letters to form a common word. Each vowel will be used only once.**

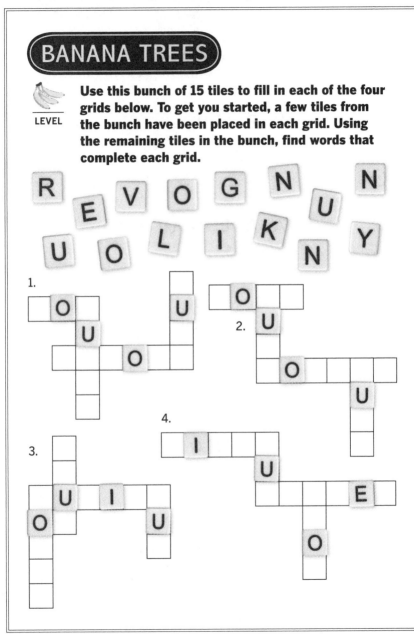

BANANA TREES

Use this bunch of 15 tiles to fill in each of the four grids below. To get you started, a few tiles from the bunch have been placed in each grid. Using the remaining tiles in the bunch, find words that complete each grid.

LEVEL

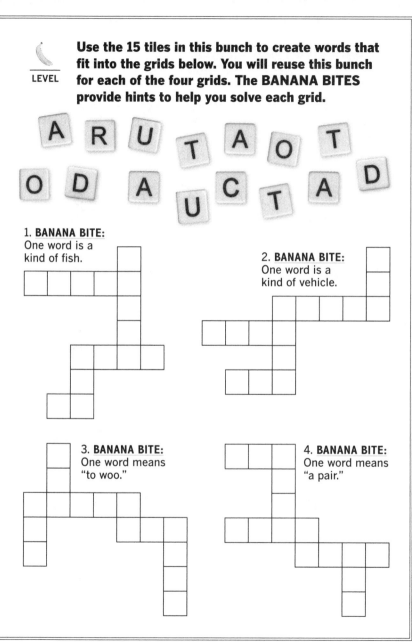

Use the 15 tiles in this bunch to create words that fit into the grids below. You will reuse this bunch for each of the four grids. The BANANA BITES provide hints to help you solve each grid.

LEVEL

A R U T A O T
O D A U C T A D

1. **BANANA BITE:**
One word is a kind of fish.

2. **BANANA BITE:**
One word is a kind of vehicle.

3. **BANANA BITE:**
One word means "to woo."

4. **BANANA BITE:**
One word means "a pair."

BANANA SHAKES

LEVEL

Each of the following seven-letter sets can be rearranged to spell out a common word that starts with I M**,** N O N **or** S E A **and/or ends with** A R Y**,** E D **or** A N T**. How quickly can you find all the words?**

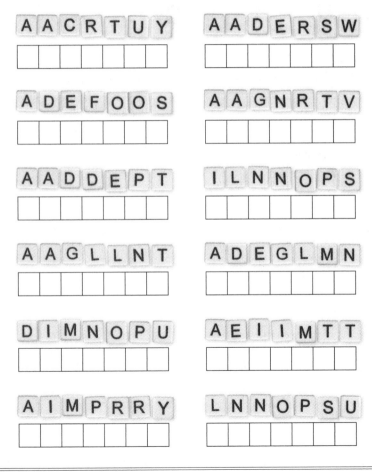

A A C R T U Y

A A D E R S W

A D E F O O S

A A G N R T V

A A D D E P T

I L N N O P S

A A G L L N T

A D E G L M N

D I M N O P U

A E I I M T T

A I M P R R Y

L N N O P S U

130

Each of the words below can be turned into another word on the list by changing one letter and then rearranging them all to form a new word. For example, REGIMENT can be turned into STEERING by changing the M to an S, so they would be a pair. How quickly can you find all the pairs?

1. AMIABLE
2. UPSTAGE
3. DECORUM
4. AIRDROP
5. SUBIDEA
6. ACRYLIC
7. MAILBAG
8. IMPLODE
9. ABUSIVE
10. VAGUEST
11. RIPCORD
12. PILOTED
13. CRUCIAL
14. RUMORED

Pairs

___ ___

___ ___

___ ___

___ ___

___ ___

___ ___

Using the 15 tiles in the bunch, fill in the spaces below according to the directions given.

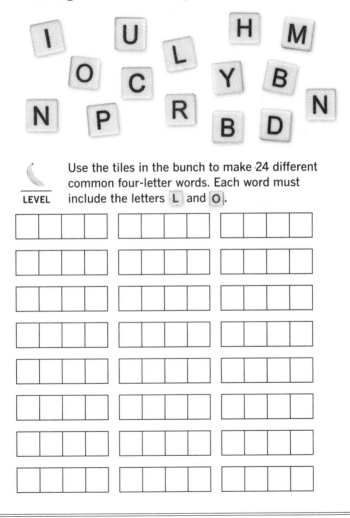

Use the tiles in the bunch to make 24 different common four-letter words. Each word must include the letters **L** and **O**.

LEVEL

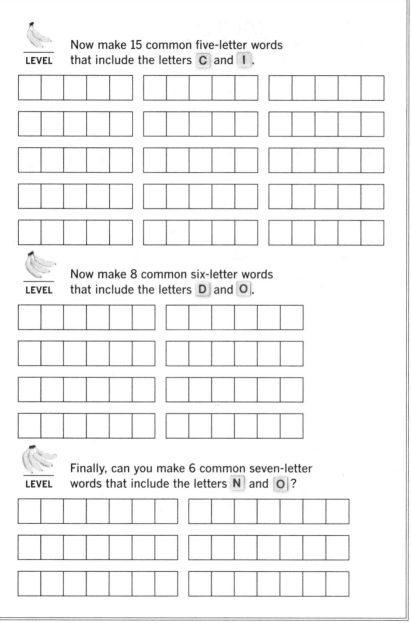

Now make 15 common five-letter words
LEVEL that include the letters C and I.

Now make 8 common six-letter words
LEVEL that include the letters D and O.

Finally, can you make 6 common seven-letter
LEVEL words that include the letters N and O?

Add an **I** to each of the words below and then rearrange the letters in each word to form a new six-letter word.

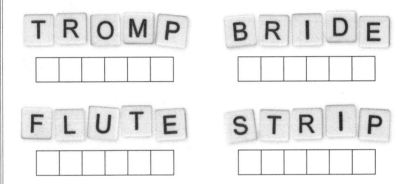

Using any letters EXCEPT the ones that appear in the bunch below, fill in the blanks to form three new words.

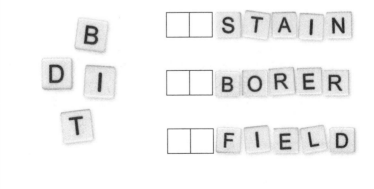

Using four of the tiles from each bunch on the left, fill in the blanks on the right to make a seven-letter word that connects the grid.

GO BANANAS!

LEVEL

Use all 21 tiles in this bunch to create a collection of connecting and intersecting common words in the grid below. The words may be horizontal or vertical, reading left to right or top to bottom.

You decide to dump a Q and draw a Z, V and V. Add them to your bunch and rearrange the words and letters in your grid as needed to form a new collection of intersecting words.

LEVEL

For each of the word groups below, change one letter in the top word to one of the letters that appears in the bottom word, then rearrange the tiles as needed to form a new common word. Do the same with each new word until you arrive at the bottom word. For example, one path from **BARK** to **PLUM** is BARK, MARK, RAMP, RUMP, PLUM.

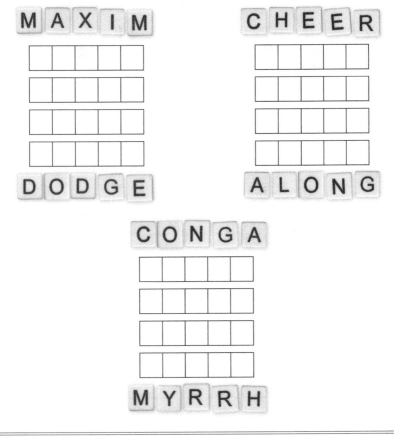

M A X I M

D O D G E

C H E E R

A L O N G

C O N G A

M Y R R H

Each of the three-letter groups below may be extended both on the right and the left to form a seven-letter word. Drawing from the tiles directly above each group, fill in the blanks to find the words as quickly as you can.

C E E G M S T

☐ ☐ L I P ☐ ☐

A C E H I N S

☐ ☐ B O O ☐ ☐

E F L N R U W

☐ ☐ A R F ☐ ☐

H I M O P R W

☐ ☐ A N T ☐ ☐

A I L L N O T

☐ ☐ L E G ☐ ☐

BANANA SPLITS

For each of the three words below, change one letter to an M **and then rearrange the letters to spell a chemical element.**

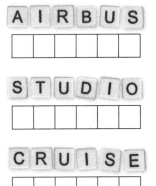

A I R B U S

☐ ☐ ☐ ☐ ☐ ☐

S T U D I O

☐ ☐ ☐ ☐ ☐ ☐

C R U I S E

☐ ☐ ☐ ☐ ☐ ☐

For each of the three words below, change one letter to a P **and then rearrange the letters to spell a type of animal.**

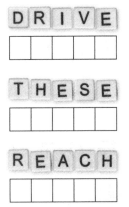

D R I V E

☐ ☐ ☐ ☐ ☐

T H E S E

☐ ☐ ☐ ☐ ☐

R E A C H

☐ ☐ ☐ ☐ ☐

Replace each of the question marks below with one of the vowels A , E , I , O **or** U **and then rearrange the letters to form a common word. Each vowel will be used only once.**

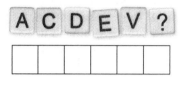

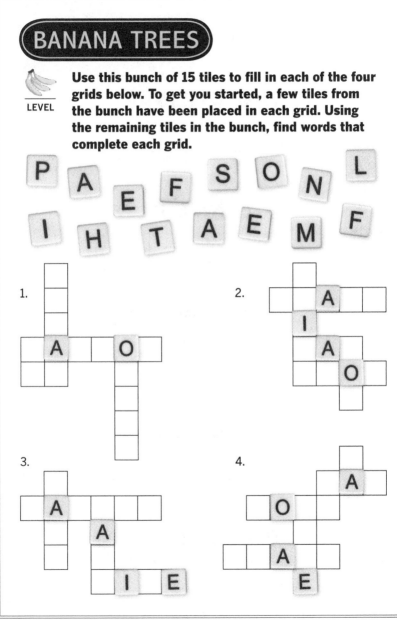

BANANA TREES

LEVEL

Use this bunch of 15 tiles to fill in each of the four grids below. To get you started, a few tiles from the bunch have been placed in each grid. Using the remaining tiles in the bunch, find words that complete each grid.

P A E F S O N L
I H T A E M F

1.

2.

3.

4.

LEVEL

Use the 15 tiles in this bunch to create words that fit into the grids below. You will reuse this bunch for each of the four grids. The BANANA BITES provide hints to help you solve each grid.

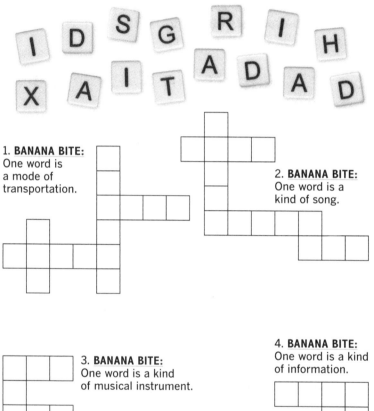

I D S G R I H
X A I T A D A D

1. **BANANA BITE:** One word is a mode of transportation.

2. **BANANA BITE:** One word is a kind of song.

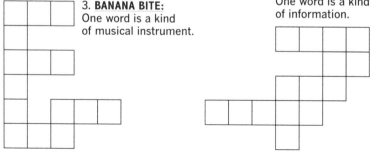

3. **BANANA BITE:** One word is a kind of musical instrument.

4. **BANANA BITE:** One word is a kind of information.

BANANA SHAKES

LEVEL

Each of the following seven-letter sets can be rearranged to spell out a common word that starts with FOR, OUT **or** CHE **and/or ends with** ED, ENT **or** ISH. **How quickly can you find all the words?**

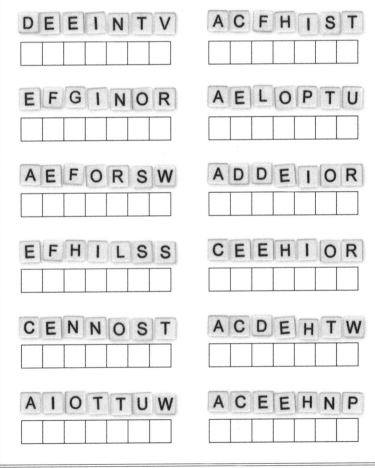

D E E I N T V

A C F H I S T

E F G I N O R

A E L O P T U

A E F O R S W

A D D E I O R

E F H I L S S

C E E H I O R

C E N N O S T

A C D E H T W

A I O T T U W

A C E E H N P

Each of the words below can be turned into another word on the list by changing one letter and then rearranging them all to form a new word. For example, REGIMENT can be turned into STEERING by changing the M to an S, so they would be a pair. How quickly can you find all the pairs?

Pairs

1. U N Y O K E D   ___ ___

2. N E W S B O Y   ___ ___

3. M O D E S T Y   ___ ___

4. H A U L A G E   ___ ___

5. I N S I G H T   ___ ___

6. S O Y B E A N   ___ ___

7. P R O D I G Y

8. V O L C A N O

9. M E T H O D S

10. N I G H T I E

11. C O O L A N T

12. D O N K E Y S

13. L A U G H E R

14. P Y G M O I D

BANANA LEAVES

Using the 15 tiles in the bunch, fill in the spaces below according to the directions given.

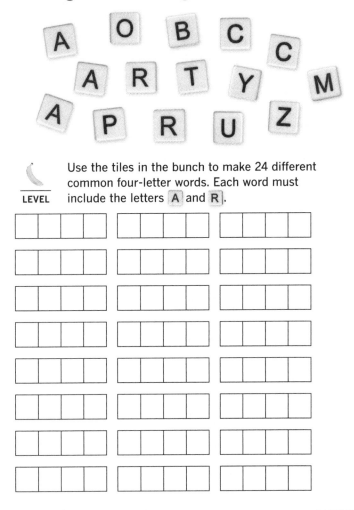

Use the tiles in the bunch to make 24 different common four-letter words. Each word must include the letters A and R.

LEVEL

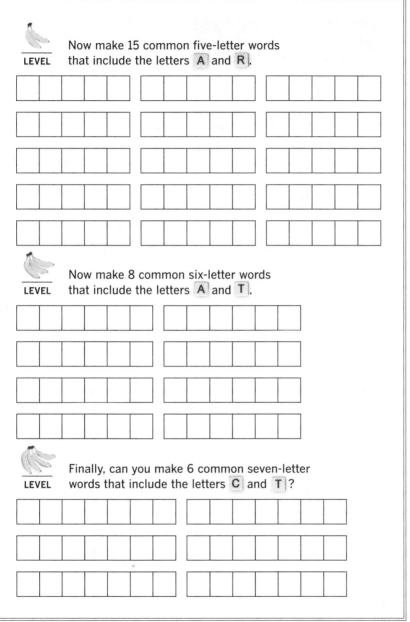

Now make 15 common five-letter words that include the letters **A** and **R**.

LEVEL

Now make 8 common six-letter words that include the letters **A** and **T**.

LEVEL

Finally, can you make 6 common seven-letter words that include the letters **C** and **T**?

LEVEL

Add a G to each of the words below and then rearrange the letters in each word to form a new six-letter word.

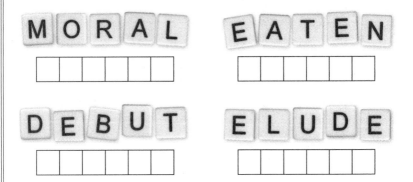

M O R A L

⬜⬜⬜⬜⬜⬜

E A T E N

⬜⬜⬜⬜⬜⬜

D E B U T

⬜⬜⬜⬜⬜⬜

E L U D E

⬜⬜⬜⬜⬜⬜

Using any letters EXCEPT the ones that appear in the bunch below, fill in the blanks to form three new words.

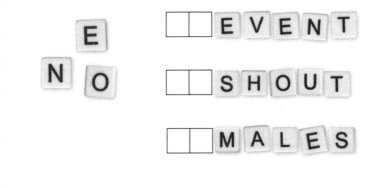

E
N O

⬜⬜ E V E N T

⬜⬜ S H O U T

⬜⬜ M A L E S

Using four of the tiles from each bunch on the left, fill in the blanks on the right to make a seven-letter word that connects the grid.

GO BANANAS!

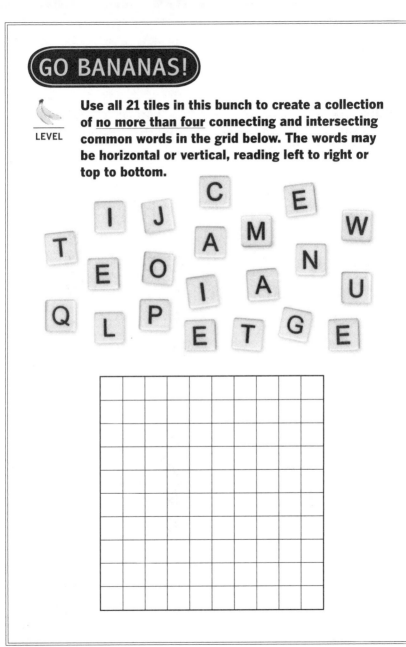

LEVEL

Use all 21 tiles in this bunch to create a collection of no more than four connecting and intersecting common words in the grid below. The words may be horizontal or vertical, reading left to right or top to bottom.

C I J A M E W

T E O I A N U

Q L P E T G E

Use all 21 tiles in this bunch to create a collection of connecting and intersecting common words in the grid below. <u>Any word that has more than two letters must be an animal.</u> The words may be horizontal or vertical, reading left to right or top to bottom.

LEVEL

LEVEL

For each of the word groups below, change one letter in the top word to one of the letters that appears in the bottom word, then rearrange the tiles as needed to form a new common word. Do the same with each new word until you arrive at the bottom word. For example, one path from **BARK** to **PLUM** is **BARK, MARK, RAMP, RUMP, PLUM.**

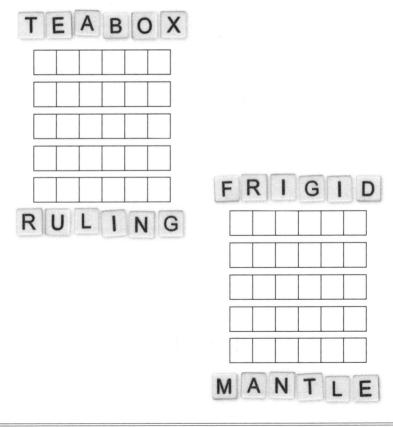

Each of the four-letter words below may be extended both on the right and the left to form an eight-letter word. Drawing from the tiles directly above each group, fill in the blanks to find the longer words as quickly as you can.

A A E I M T V
[ ][ ] B R O S [ ][ ]

E G N O P R U
[ ][ ] A N D S [ ][ ]

F I M N R T U
[ ][ ] L A M E [ ][ ]

A H I N R T Y
[ ][ ] D U S T [ ][ ]

C D E G N O T
[ ][ ] H E R E [ ][ ]

BANANA SPLITS

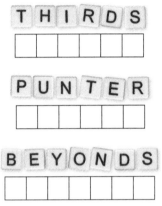

LEVEL

For each of the three words below, change one letter to an A and then rearrange the letters to spell a type of food.

T H I R D S

P U N T E R

B E Y O N D S

For each of the three words below, change one letter to an M and then rearrange the letters to spell the name of a city.

R A I D E D

B A R I U M

T O L E R A N T

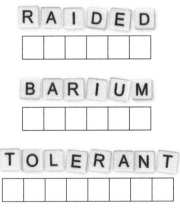

Replace each of the question marks below with one of the vowels A, E, I, O or U and then rearrange the letters to form a common word. Each vowel will be used only once.

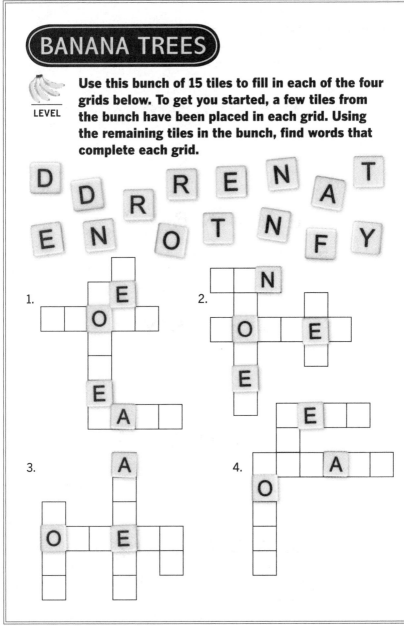

BANANA TREES

LEVEL

Use this bunch of 15 tiles to fill in each of the four grids below. To get you started, a few tiles from the bunch have been placed in each grid. Using the remaining tiles in the bunch, find words that complete each grid.

D D R R E N A T
E N O T N F Y

1. E O E A

2. N O E E

3. A O E

4. E A O

LEVEL

Use the 15 tiles in this bunch to create words that fit into the grids below. You will reuse this bunch for each of the four grids. The BANANA BITES provide hints to help you solve each grid.

A A E E I O O W
G J K M S T R

1. **BANANA BITE:** One word is a Southern staple.

2. **BANANA BITE:** One word is a sound an animal makes.

3. **BANANA BITE:** One word means "an error."

4. **BANANA BITE:** One word is a kind of animal.

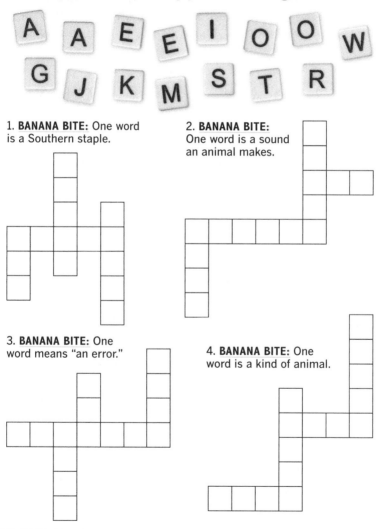

157

LEVEL

Each of the following seven-letter sets can be rearranged to spell out a common word that starts with O U, O V or S T and/or ends with E T, F Y or N T. How quickly can you find all the words?

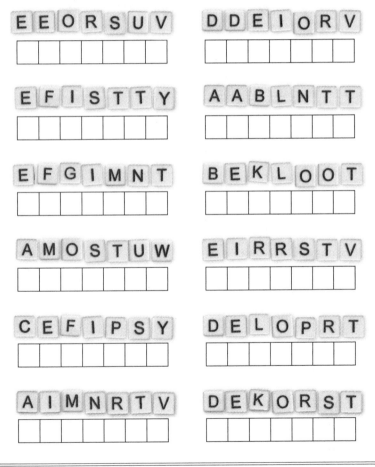

E E O R S U V

D D E I O R V

E F I S T T Y

A A B L N T T

E F G I M N T

B E K L O O T

A M O S T U W

E I R R S T V

C E F I P S Y

D E L O P R T

A I M N R T V

D E K O R S T

Each of the words below can be turned into another word on the list by changing one letter and then rearranging them all to form a new word. For example, REGIMENT can be turned into STEERING by changing the M to an S, so they would be a pair. How quickly can you find all the pairs?

Pairs

1. B A C H E L O R

__ __

2. A N Y P L A C E

__ __

3. H E R O I C A L

— —

4. L O C A L I S E

__ __

5. V A G A R I E S

— —

6. P A R L A N C E

— —

7. B R A I N I A C

8. P I T T A N C E

9. C I N N A B A R

10. J A U N D I C E

11. A B R A S I V E

12. T E N A C I T Y

13. C O L E S L A W

14. G U I D A N C E

BANANA LEAVES

Using the 15 tiles in the bunch, fill in the spaces below according to the directions given.

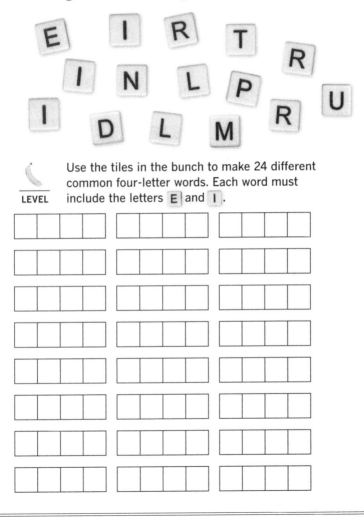

LEVEL

Use the tiles in the bunch to make 24 different common four-letter words. Each word must include the letters E and I.

160

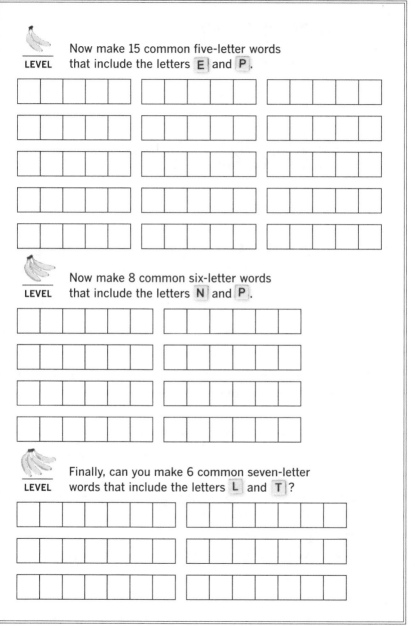

LEVEL Now make 15 common five-letter words that include the letters E and P.

LEVEL Now make 8 common six-letter words that include the letters N and P.

LEVEL Finally, can you make 6 common seven-letter words that include the letters L and T?

BANANA FILLING

LEVEL

Add a **C** to each of the words below and then rearrange the letters in each word to form a new six-letter word.

A R E N A

☐☐☐☐☐☐

P A I N T

☐☐☐☐☐☐

S O A R S

☐☐☐☐☐☐

A T O N E

☐☐☐☐☐☐

Using any letters EXCEPT the ones that appear in the bunch below, fill in the blanks to form three new words.

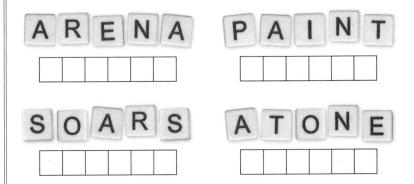

B

D   E

R   U

☐☐ S T I F F S

☐☐ W E L L E D

☐☐ R E N T A L

Using four of the tiles from each bunch on the left, fill in the blanks on the right to make a seven-letter word that connects the grid.

GO BANANAS!

LEVEL

Use all 21 tiles in this bunch to create a collection of <u>no more than four</u> connecting and intersecting common words in the grid below. The words may be horizontal or vertical, reading left to right or top to bottom.

Use all 21 tiles in this bunch to create a collection of connecting and intersecting common words in the grid below. <u>Any word that has more than two letters must be one of the United States.</u> The words may be horizontal or vertical, reading left to right or top to bottom.

BANANA BOATS

LEVEL

For each of the word groups below, change one letter in the top word to one of the letters that appears in the bottom word, then rearrange the tiles as needed to form a new common word. Do the same with each new word until you arrive at the bottom word. For example, one path from BARK to PLUM is BARK, MARK, RAMP, RUMP, PLUM.

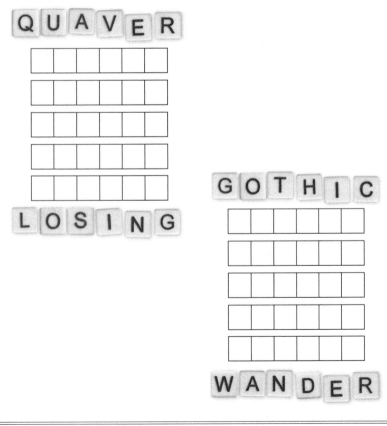

QUAVER

LOSING

GOTHIC

WANDER

Each of the four-letter words below may be extended both on the right and the left to form an eight-letter word. Drawing from the tiles directly above each group, fill in the blanks to find the longer words as quickly as you can.

D E G L O T U

☐ ☐ I M P S ☐ ☐

A B C E L T Y

☐ ☐ T O R N ☐ ☐

A B C G H I M

☐ ☐ T A C O ☐ ☐

E H M N O R S

☐ ☐ T H O U ☐ ☐

A B B E L M T

☐ ☐ T H R O ☐ ☐

LEVEL

For each of the three words below, change one letter to a T **and then rearrange the letters to spell a type of animal.**

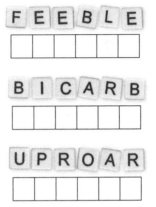

F E E B L E

B I C A R B

U P R O A R

For each of the three words below, change one letter to an R **and then rearrange the letters to spell a part of the body.**

F E T I N G

M A T U R E D

N U M B E S T

Replace each of the question marks below with one of the vowels A, E, I, O or U and then rearrange the letters to form a common word. Each vowel will be used only once.

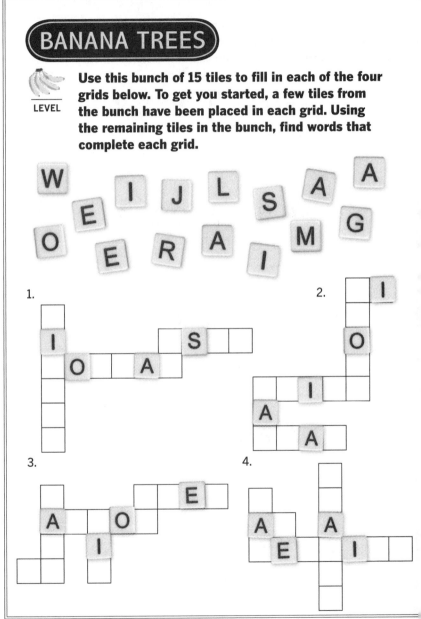

BANANA TREES

LEVEL

Use this bunch of 15 tiles to fill in each of the four grids below. To get you started, a few tiles from the bunch have been placed in each grid. Using the remaining tiles in the bunch, find words that complete each grid.

W E I J L S A A
O E R A I M G

1.
2.
3.
4.

Use the 15 tiles in this bunch to create words that fit into the grids below. You will reuse this bunch for each of the four grids. The BANANA BITES provide hints to help you solve each grid.

LEVEL

A E I O L N R V E E I O M H T

1. **BANANA BITE:** One word means "to perfect."

2. **BANANA BITE:** One word is a kind of poison.

3. **BANANA BITE:** One word is a measure of distance.

4. **BANANA BITE:** One word is a baseball term.

BANANA SHAKES

LEVEL

Each of the following seven-letter sets can be rearranged to spell out a common word that starts with A B , M I or O U and/or ends with L E , N E or I D . How quickly can you find all the words?

D E I I L M N

A D E I M R Y

A K L O T T U

A D D I N O R

A B E L O S V

A B D I L O T

O O O R T T U

A B C D N O S

C E I I N S U

A E G I I M N

A B B E L U Y

A A B E L P Y

Each of the words below can be turned into another word on the list by changing one letter and then rearranging them all to form a new word. For example, REGIMENT can be turned into STEERING by changing the M to an S, so they would be a pair. How quickly can you find all the pairs?

Pairs

1. F L A M I N G O

2. D R I F T A G E ___ ___

3. W A R T I M E S ___ ___

4. M A N I F O L D ___ ___

5. L A D Y L I K E ___ ___

6. R A T I F I E D ___ ___

7. M A D H O U S E ___ ___

8. T A P E S T R Y

9. F A C T O T U M

10. S W I M W E A R

11. O U T M A T C H

12. A M B U S H E D

13. P R O S T A T E

14. M E D I A L L Y

BANANA LEAVES

Using the 15 tiles in the bunch, fill in the spaces below according to the directions given.

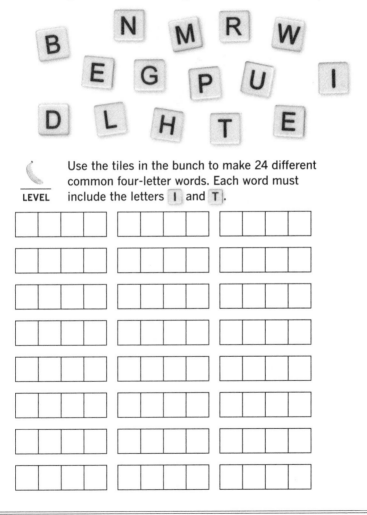

Use the tiles in the bunch to make 24 different common four-letter words. Each word must include the letters **I** and **T**.

LEVEL

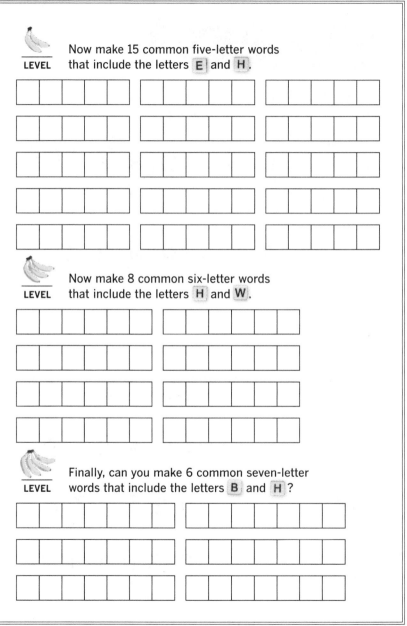

LEVEL Now make 15 common five-letter words that include the letters **E** and **H**.

LEVEL Now make 8 common six-letter words that include the letters **H** and **W**.

LEVEL Finally, can you make 6 common seven-letter words that include the letters **B** and **H**?

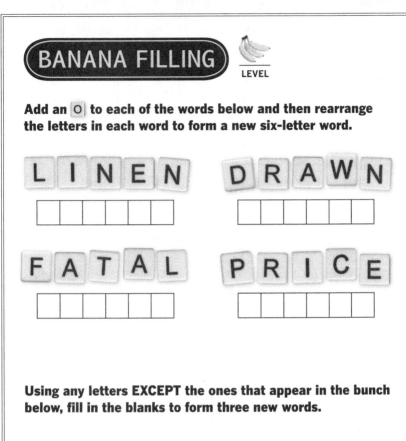

Add an O **to each of the words below and then rearrange the letters in each word to form a new six-letter word.**

L I N E N

D R A W N

F A T A L

P R I C E

Using any letters EXCEPT the ones that appear in the bunch below, fill in the blanks to form three new words.

O

U

⬚⬚ L I N G E R

⬚⬚ D E R A T E

⬚⬚ S A N I T Y

Using four of the tiles from each bunch on the left, fill in the blanks on the right to make a seven-letter word that connects the grid.

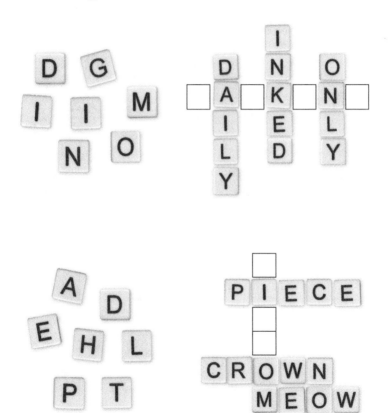

GO BANANAS!

LEVEL

Use all 21 tiles in this bunch to create a collection of connecting and intersecting common words in the grid below. <u>Any word that has more than two letters must be a chemical element.</u> The words may be horizontal or vertical, reading left to right or top to bottom.

LEVEL

Use all 21 tiles in this bunch to create a collection of connecting and intersecting common words in the grid below. **Each word must contain at least six letters.** The words may be horizontal or vertical, reading left to right or top to bottom.

179

For each of the word groups below, change one letter in the top word to one of the letters that appears in the bottom word, then rearrange the tiles as needed to form a new common word. Do the same with each new word until you arrive at the bottom word. For example, one path from **BARK** to **PLUM** is **BARK, MARK, RAMP, RUMP, PLUM.**

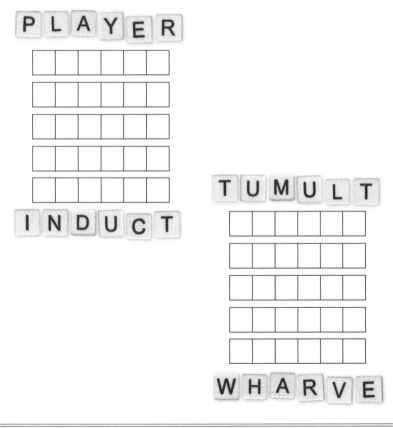

Each of the four-letter words below may be extended both on the right and the left to form an eight-letter word. Drawing from the tiles directly above each group, fill in the blanks to find the longer words as quickly as you can.

B E N O R T V

☐ ☐ S O L E ☐ ☐

A F H L M O R

☐ ☐ S P I T ☐ ☐

I O P S S T U

☐ ☐ L I N E ☐ ☐

A C I L O P T

☐ ☐ L O S S ☐ ☐

A B C E L R U

☐ ☐ M I S O ☐ ☐

For each of the three words below, change one letter to an R and then rearrange the letters to spell a type of furniture.

D E S I R E S

R O M A I N E

S I L E N C E R

For each of the three words below, change one letter to an O and then rearrange the letters to spell the last name of a U.S. president.

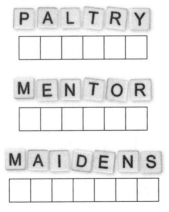

P A L T R Y

M E N T O R

M A I D E N S

Replace each of the question marks below with one of the vowels A , E , I , O **or** U **and then rearrange the letters to form a common word. Each vowel will be used only once.**

A A C G L T ?

C D I L O R ?

A A B D G N ?

A E N P T T ?

A I L S T W ?

183

BANANA TREES

LEVEL

Use this bunch of 15 tiles to fill in each of the four grids below. To get you started, a few tiles from the bunch have been placed in each grid. Using the remaining tiles in the bunch, find words that complete each grid.

Tiles: O, E, A, E, S, K, W, T, U, E, I, S, D, P, D

1.

2.

3.

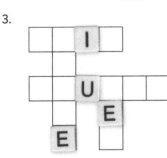

4.

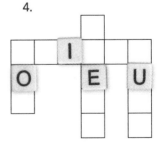

LEVEL

Use the 15 tiles in this bunch to create words that fit into the grids below. You will reuse this bunch for each of the four grids. The BANANA BITES provide hints to help you solve each grid.

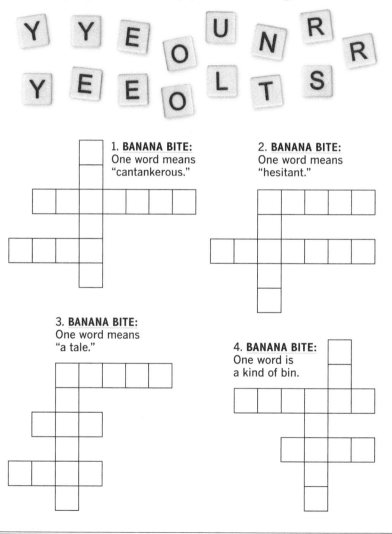

Y Y YE O U N R R Y E E O L T S

1. BANANA BITE:
One word means
"cantankerous."

2. BANANA BITE:
One word means
"hesitant."

3. BANANA BITE:
One word means
"a tale."

4. BANANA BITE:
One word is
a kind of bin.

185

BANANA SHAKES

LEVEL

Each of the following seven-letter sets can be rearranged to spell out a common word that starts with `R E`, `O V` **or** `U N` **and/or ends with** `A L`, `V E` **or** `E S`. **How quickly can you find all the words?**

A A B L M S Y

A C D E I N S

B D E I O R V

E E E O R S V

E E I L S U V

A A C D I L R

A E F I N R R

A D E I I S S

C E I N N O V

A D E N P U V

A C H I N N U

A E E L N R W

Each of the words below can be turned into another word on the list by changing one letter and then rearranging them all to form a new word. For example, REGIMENT can be turned into STEERING by changing the M to an S, so they would be a pair. How quickly can you find all the pairs?

Pairs

1. OUTGLARE
___ ___

2. COVENANT
___ ___

3. HUSBANDS
___ ___

4. HOSPITAL
___ ___

5. CAMOMILE
___ ___

6. WATERLOG
___ ___

7. HEADLINE

8. SUNSHADE

9. SNAPSHOT

10. DENIABLE

11. NANOTECH

12. MEMORIAL

13. ASTONISH

14. SHOPLIFT

BANANA LEAVES

Using the 15 tiles in the bunch, fill in the spaces below according to the directions given.

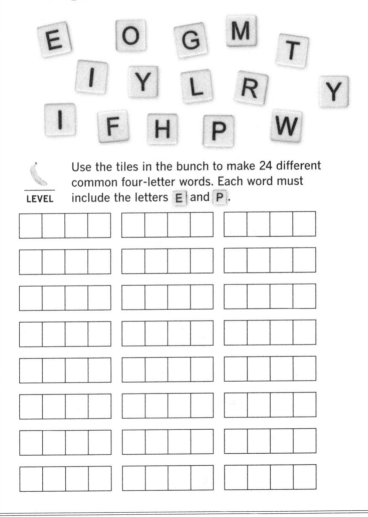

E O G M T I Y L R Y I F H P W

Use the tiles in the bunch to make 24 different common four-letter words. Each word must include the letters E and P.

LEVEL

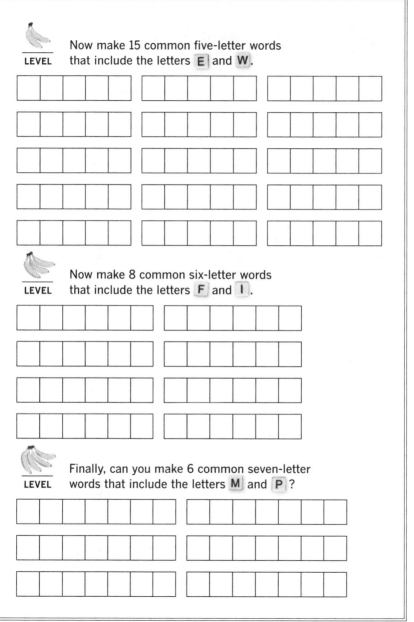

Now make 15 common five-letter words that include the letters **E** and **W**.

LEVEL

Now make 8 common six-letter words that include the letters **F** and **I**.

LEVEL

Finally, can you make 6 common seven-letter words that include the letters **M** and **P**?

LEVEL

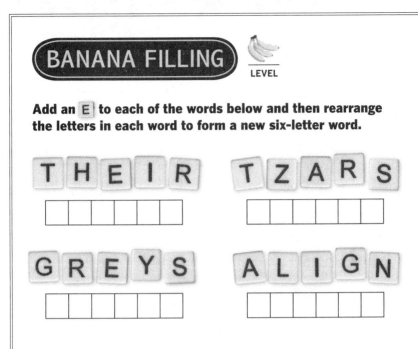

BANANA FILLING

Add an **E** to each of the words below and then rearrange the letters in each word to form a new six-letter word.

THEIR

⬜⬜⬜⬜⬜⬜

TZARS

⬜⬜⬜⬜⬜⬜

GREYS

⬜⬜⬜⬜⬜⬜

ALIGN

⬜⬜⬜⬜⬜⬜

Using any letters EXCEPT the ones that appear in the bunch below, fill in the blanks to form three new words.

⬜⬜ CURATE

V P

⬜⬜ LANCES

⬜⬜ SWORDS

Using four of the tiles from each bunch on the left, fill in the blanks on the right to make a seven-letter word that connects the grid.

GO BANANAS!

LEVEL

Use all 21 tiles in this bunch to create a collection of <u>no more than four</u> connecting and intersecting common words in the grid below. The words may be horizontal or vertical, reading left to right or top to bottom.

LEVEL

Use all 21 tiles in this bunch to create a collection of connecting and intersecting common words in the grid below. <u>Each word must contain at least six letters.</u> The words may be horizontal or vertical, reading left to right or top to bottom.

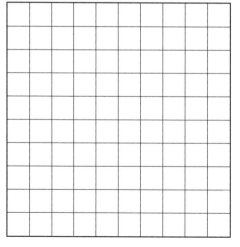

BANANA BOATS

LEVEL

For each of the word groups below, change one letter in the top word to one of the letters that appears in the bottom word, then rearrange the tiles as needed to form a new common word. Do the same with each new word until you arrive at the bottom word. For example, one path from **BARK** to **PLUM** is BARK, MARK, RAMP, RUMP, PLUM.

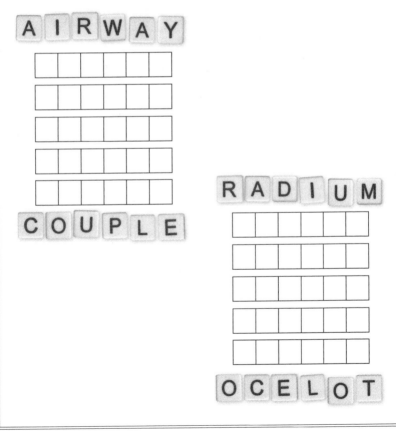

A I R W A Y

C O U P L E

R A D I U M

O C E L O T

194

Each of the four-letter words below may be extended both on the right and the left to form an eight-letter word. Drawing from the tiles directly above each group, fill in the blanks to find the longer words as quickly as you can.

C E H I O O T

☐ ☐ R E I N ☐ ☐

A D E G O P R

☐ ☐ R A N G ☐ ☐

E E H I L N P

☐ ☐ T A N G ☐ ☐

B D E E I K N

☐ ☐ R O S E ☐ ☐

E E L N O S T

☐ ☐ G A L E ☐ ☐

BANANA SPLITS

For each of the three words below, change one letter to an **H** and then rearrange the letters to spell a type of flower.

C A R D I O

L O W L Y

Y A C H T I N G

For each of the three words below, change one letter to a **T** and then rearrange the letters to spell a part of the body.

E N O U G H

A U T H O R

C H A M O I S

196

Replace each of the question marks below with one of the vowels A **,** E **,** I **,** O **or** U **and then rearrange the letters to form a common word. Each vowel will be used only once.**

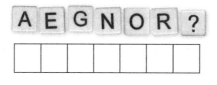

BANANA TREES

LEVEL

Use this bunch of 15 tiles to fill in each of the four grids below. To get you started, a few tiles from the bunch have been placed in each grid. Using the remaining tiles in the bunch, find words that complete each grid.

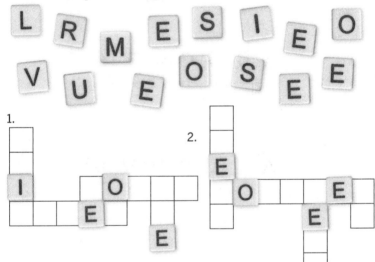

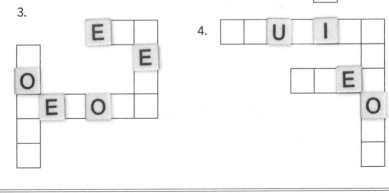

Use the 15 tiles in this bunch to create words that fit into the grids below. You will reuse this bunch for each of the four grids. The BANANA BITES provide hints to help you solve each grid.

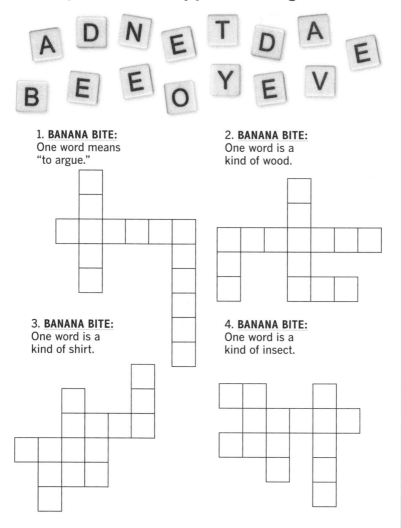

A D N E T D A E
B E E O Y E V

1. **BANANA BITE:**
One word means "to argue."

2. **BANANA BITE:**
One word is a kind of wood.

3. **BANANA BITE:**
One word is a kind of shirt.

4. **BANANA BITE:**
One word is a kind of insect.

BANANA SHAKES

LEVEL

Each of the following seven-letter sets can be rearranged to spell out a common word that either starts with `P R`**,** `U P`**, or** `E X` **and/or ends with** `S T`**,** `K E`**, or** `U M`**. How quickly can you find all the words?**

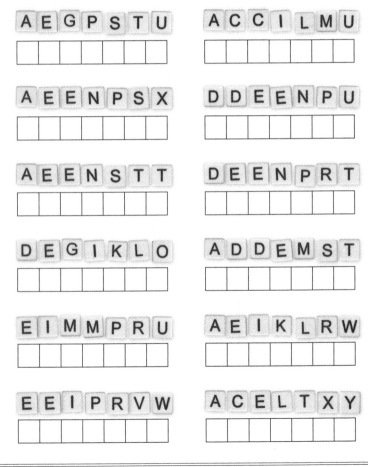

`A E G P S T U`

`A C C I L M U`

`A E E N P S X`

`D D E E N P U`

`A E E N S T T`

`D E E N P R T`

`D E G I K L O`

`A D D E M S T`

`E I M M P R U`

`A E I K L R W`

`E E I P R V W`

`A C E L T X Y`

Each of the words below can be turned into another word on the list by changing one letter and then rearranging them all to form a new word. For example, REGIMENT can be turned into STEERING by changing the M to an S, so they would be a pair. How quickly can you find all the pairs?

Pairs

1. ORGANIST
2. HOOLIGAN
3. TEMPORAL
4. PITCHMAN
5. IMPERIAL
6. ADHESION
7. GRAFFITI
8. LONGHAIR
9. GOATSKIN
10. AFFRIGHT
11. NIGHTCAP
12. PLETHORA
13. DEANSHIP
14. PRIMEVAL

___ ___
___ ___
___ ___
___ ___
___ ___
___ ___

BANANA LEAVES

Using the 15 tiles in the bunch, fill in the spaces below according to the directions given.

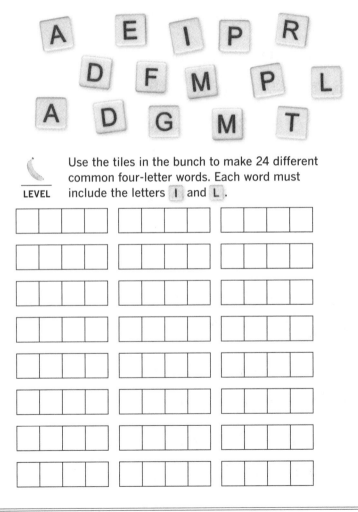

Use the tiles in the bunch to make 24 different common four-letter words. Each word must include the letters **I** and **L**.

LEVEL

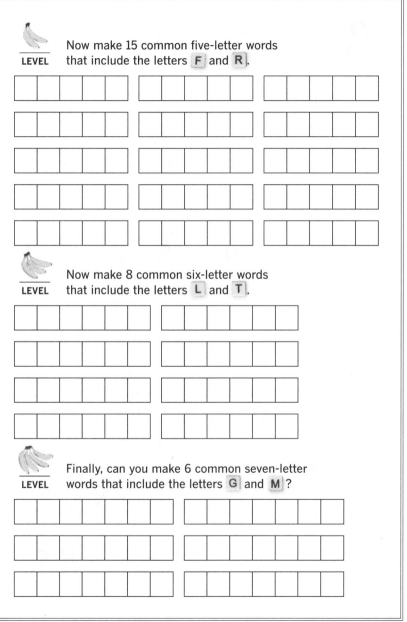

Now make 15 common five-letter words that include the letters **F** and **R**.

LEVEL

Now make 8 common six-letter words that include the letters **L** and **T**.

LEVEL

Finally, can you make 6 common seven-letter words that include the letters **G** and **M**?

LEVEL

BANANA FILLING

Add an **F** to each of the words below and then rearrange the letters in each word to form a new six-letter word.

A C U T E

☐ ☐ ☐ ☐ ☐ ☐

R O V E R

☐ ☐ ☐ ☐ ☐ ☐

A R I A S

☐ ☐ ☐ ☐ ☐ ☐

S H I F T

☐ ☐ ☐ ☐ ☐ ☐

Using any letters EXCEPT the ones that appear in the bunch below, fill in the blanks to form three new words.

E

N

☐ ☐ G R A T E S

☐ ☐ T R A N K S

☐ ☐ F E L I N E

Using four of the tiles from each bunch on the left, fill in the blanks on the right to make a seven-letter word that connects the grid.

GO BANANAS!

LEVEL

Use all 21 tiles in this bunch to create a collection of connecting and intersecting common words in the grid below. <u>Any word that has more than two letters must be a thing found in a school.</u> The words may be horizontal or vertical, reading left to right or top to bottom.

Use all 21 tiles in this bunch to create a collection of connecting and intersecting common words in the grid below. **Each word must contain at least six letters.** The words may be horizontal or vertical, reading left to right or top to bottom.

LEVEL

BANANA BOATS

LEVEL

For each of the word groups below, change one letter in the top word to one of the letters that appears in the bottom word, then rearrange the tiles as needed to form a new common word. Do the same with each new word until you arrive at the bottom word. For example, one path from **BARK** to **PLUM** is **BARK, MARK, RAMP, RUMP, PLUM.**

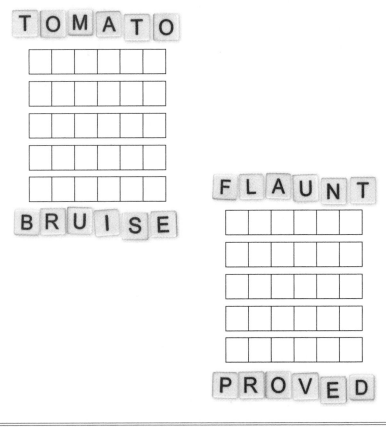

TOMATO

BRUISE

FLAUNT

PROVED

Each of the four-letter words below may be extended both on the right and the left to form an eight-letter word. Drawing from the tiles directly above each group, fill in the blanks to find the longer words as quickly as you can.

A C E H L M R

⬚ ⬚ V E N D ⬚ ⬚

A I N N R T W

⬚ ⬚ S O L E ⬚ ⬚

A B O S S T U

⬚ ⬚ N I N E ⬚ ⬚

A A C G I M R

⬚ ⬚ L E N D ⬚ ⬚

A E I N O P T

⬚ ⬚ P A R E ⬚ ⬚

BANANA SPLITS

LEVEL

For each of the three words below, change one letter to an R and then rearrange the letters to spell a type of dog.

R E W R I T E

⬜⬜⬜⬜⬜⬜⬜

E S T A T E

⬜⬜⬜⬜⬜⬜

A D O R A B L E

⬜⬜⬜⬜⬜⬜⬜⬜

For each of the three words below, change one letter to an I and then rearrange the letters to spell a word related to math.

T R O L L I N G

⬜⬜⬜⬜⬜⬜⬜

C L A M P E D

⬜⬜⬜⬜⬜⬜⬜

T H R E A T E N

⬜⬜⬜⬜⬜⬜⬜⬜

Replace each of the question marks below with one of the vowels A, E, I, O or U **and then rearrange the letters to form a common word. Each vowel will be used only once.**

BANANA TREES

LEVEL

Use this bunch of 15 tiles to fill in each of the four grids below. To get you started, a few tiles from the bunch have been placed in each grid. Using the remaining tiles in the bunch, find words that complete each grid.

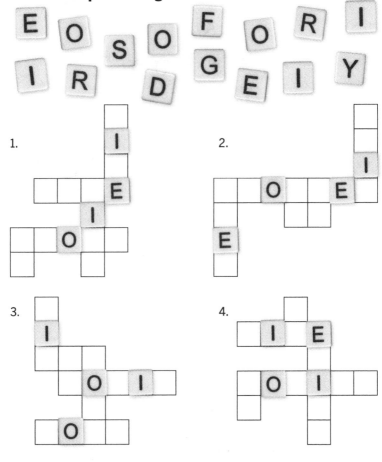

Use the **15 tiles in this bunch to create words that fit into the grids below. You will reuse this bunch for each of the four grids. The BANANA BITES provide hints to help you solve each grid.**

LEVEL

A C O F T J N Y I O A B N V W

1. BANANA BITE:
One word is a kind of musical instrument.

2. BANANA BITE:
One word is a kind of coffee.

3. BANANA BITE:
One word is a kind of vehicle.

4. BANANA BITE:
One word is a body of water.

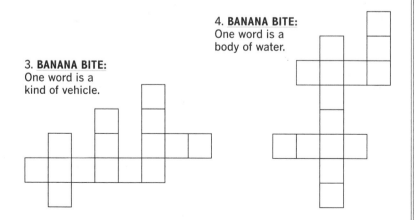

213

BANANA SHAKES

LEVEL

Each of the following seven-letter sets can be rearranged to spell out a common word that either starts with D I, E N, or I N and/or ends with I C, G E, or N E. How quickly can you find all the words?

A E F N O P R

A A E G M P R

A E E F L M N

A H I M N N U

A E E H M N T

A C E G O R U

A D D I I N S

A C D I R S T

C E N P R T Y

B D E I O S Y

B H I I I N T

A A C C H I R

214

Each of the words below can be turned into another word on the list by changing one letter and then rearranging them all to form a new word. For example, REGIMENT can be turned into STEERING by changing the M to an S, so they would be a pair. How quickly can you find all the pairs?

Pairs
___ ___
___ ___
___ ___
___ ___
___ ___
___ ___
___ ___

1. ENTHUSED
2. ADHESIVE
3. PAVILION
4. DEMONISE
5. INTUITED
6. DOVETAIL
7. DISHEVEL
8. DINGHIES
9. NOSEDIVE
10. FIENDISH
11. VISIONAL
12. IDENTITY
13. ADOPTIVE
14. SLEUTHED

215

BANANA LEAVES

Using the 15 tiles in the bunch, fill in the spaces below according to the directions given.

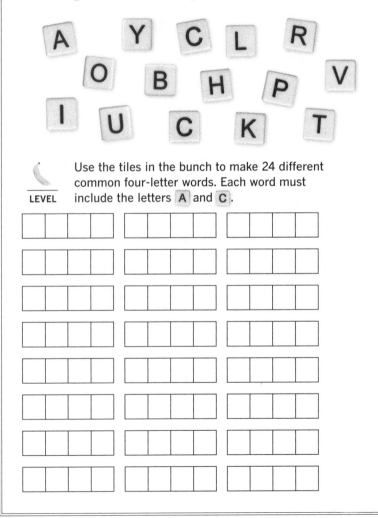

Use the tiles in the bunch to make 24 different common four-letter words. Each word must include the letters A and C.

LEVEL

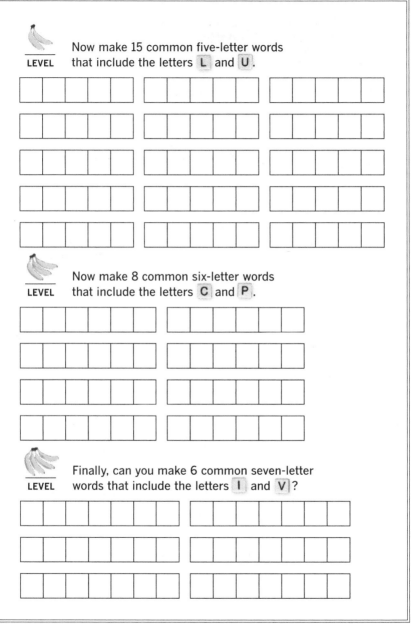

LEVEL Now make 15 common five-letter words that include the letters **L** and **U**.

LEVEL Now make 8 common six-letter words that include the letters **C** and **P**.

LEVEL Finally, can you make 6 common seven-letter words that include the letters **I** and **V**?

BANANA FILLING

LEVEL

Add a W **to each of the words below and then rearrange the letters in each word to form a new six-letter word.**

R E L A Y

L I M E D

L I V E S

B E S O T

Using any letters EXCEPT the ones that appear in the bunch below, fill in the blanks to form three new words.

E

U

☐ ☐ S O L U T E

☐ ☐ B O U N D S

☐ ☐ S L I N G S

Using four of the tiles from each bunch on the left, fill in the blanks on the right to make a seven-letter word that connects the grid.

GO BANANAS!

LEVEL

Use all 21 tiles in this bunch to create a collection of <u>no more than four</u> connecting and intersecting common words in the grid below. The words may be horizontal or vertical, reading left to right or top to bottom.

LEVEL

Use all 21 tiles in this bunch to create a collection of connecting and intersecting common words in the grid below. **Each word must contain at least six letters.** The words may be horizontal or vertical, reading left to right or top to bottom.

LEVEL

For each of the word groups below, change one letter in the top word to one of the letters that appears in the bottom word, then rearrange the tiles as needed to form a new common word. Do the same with each new word until you arrive at the bottom word. For example, one path from **BARK** to **PLUM** is BARK, MARK, RAMP, RUMP, PLUM.

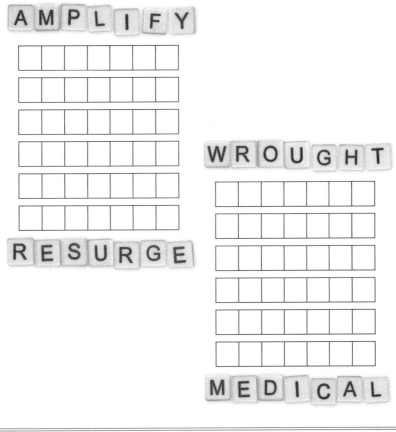

A M P L I F Y

R E S U R G E

W R O U G H T

M E D I C A L

Each of the three-letter groups below may be extended both on the right and the left to form a nine-letter word. Drawing from the tiles directly above each group, fill in the blanks to find the words as quickly as you can.

A D I L N S T

☐ ☐ ☐ S O N ☐ ☐ ☐

A A C I M N T

☐ ☐ ☐ T I C ☐ ☐ ☐

A E E G N T V

☐ ☐ ☐ T I L ☐ ☐ ☐

E E I L M P Z

☐ ☐ ☐ H A S ☐ ☐ ☐

A C I L N O R

☐ ☐ ☐ L E G ☐ ☐ ☐

For each of the three words below, change one letter to a T and then rearrange the letters to spell a mode of transportation.

C H O K E R

L O Y A L E R

A L B A C O R E S

For each of the three words below, change one letter to an N and then rearrange the letters to spell a type of bird.

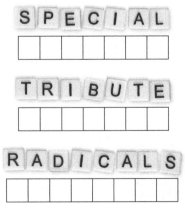

S P E C I A L

T R I B U T E

R A D I C A L S

Replace each of the question marks below with one of the vowels A, E, I, O or U and then rearrange the letters to form a common word. Each vowel will be used only once.

A C E E G L N ?

A A B E L T T ?

A B L M N O R ?

B B N R S T U ?

A B E G L O T ?

BANANA TREES

LEVEL

Use this bunch of 15 tiles to fill in each of the four grids below. To get you started, a few tiles from the bunch have been placed in each grid. Using the remaining tiles in the bunch, find words that complete each grid.

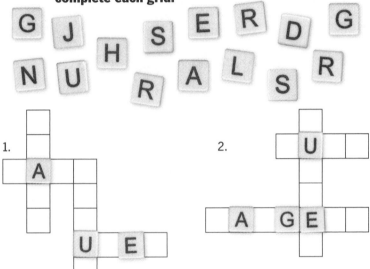

G J H S E R D G
N U R A L S R

1.

A

U E

2.

U

A G E

3.

A

U E

4.

A

U E

S

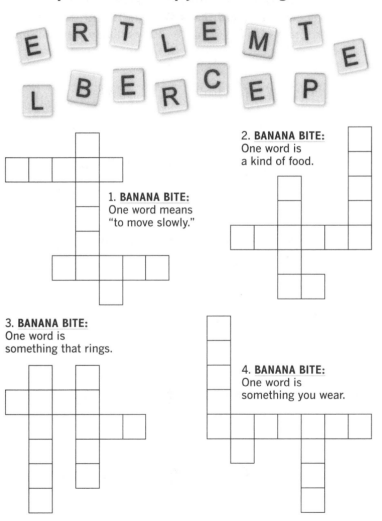

Use the 15 tiles in this bunch to create words that fit into the grids below. You will reuse this bunch for each of the four grids. The BANANA BITES provide hints to help you solve each grid.

LEVEL

E R T L E M T E
L B E R C E P

2. BANANA BITE:
One word is a kind of food.

1. BANANA BITE:
One word means "to move slowly."

3. BANANA BITE:
One word is something that rings.

4. BANANA BITE:
One word is something you wear.

BANANA SHAKES

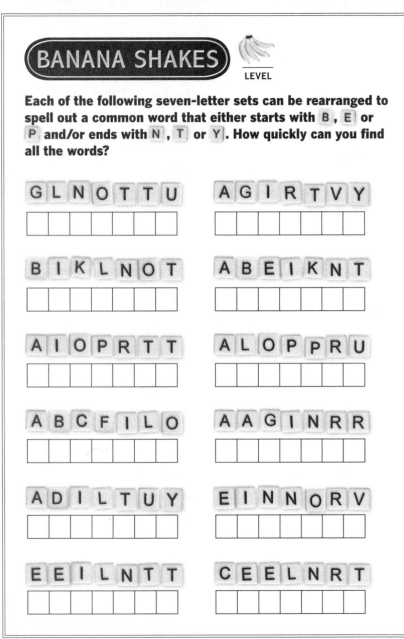

LEVEL

Each of the following seven-letter sets can be rearranged to spell out a common word that either starts with B, E or P and/or ends with N, T or Y. How quickly can you find all the words?

G L N O T T U

A G I R T V Y

B I K L N O T

A B E I K N T

A I O P R T T

A L O P P R U

A B C F I L O

A A G I N R R

A D I L T U Y

E I N N O R V

E E I L N T T

C E E L N R T

228

Each of the words below can be turned into another word on the list by changing one letter and then rearranging them all to form a new word. For example, REGIMENT can be turned into STEERING by changing the M to an S, so they would be a pair. How quickly can you find all the pairs?

Pairs

1. M I S M A N A G E ___ ___

2. M A L F O R M E D ___ ___

3. E N C H I L A D A ___ ___

4. F I R M A M E N T ___ ___

5. P A R A M E T E R ___ ___

6. S A N D B L A S T ___ ___

7. M E L O D R A M A

8. H A C I E N D A S

9. U P S A D A I S Y

10. M A I N F R A M E

11. C A B S T A N D S

12. D Y S P L A S I A

13. M A G N E S I U M

14. P R E M A T U R E

BANANA LEAVES

Using the 15 tiles in the bunch, fill in the spaces below according to the directions given.

Use the tiles in the bunch to make 24 different common four-letter words. Each word must include the letters **D** and **E**.

LEVEL

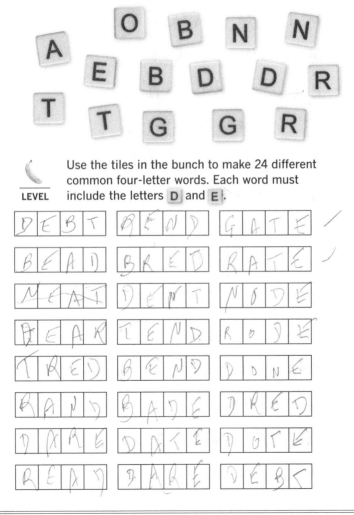

D	E	B	T		B	E	N	D		G	A	T	E
B	E	A	D		B	R	E	D		R	A	T	E
M	E	A	T		D	E	N	T		N	O	D	E
H	E	A	R		L	E	N	D		R	O	D	E
T	R	E	D		B	E	N	D		D	O	N	E
B	A	N	D		B	A	D	E		D	R	E	D
D	A	R	E		D	A	T	E		D	O	T	E
R	E	A	D		D	A	R	E		D	E	B	S

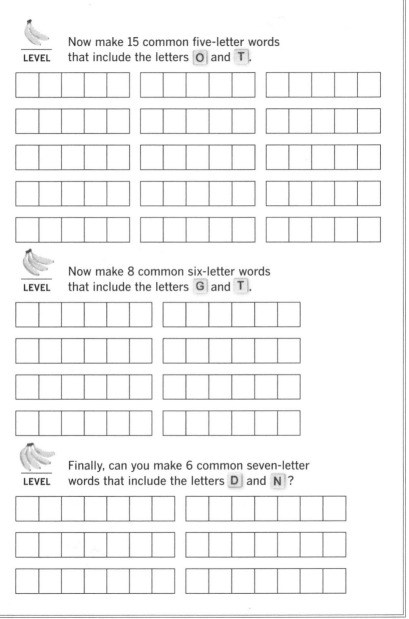

LEVEL Now make 15 common five-letter words that include the letters **O** and **T**.

LEVEL Now make 8 common six-letter words that include the letters **G** and **T**.

LEVEL Finally, can you make 6 common seven-letter words that include the letters **D** and **N**?

BANANA FILLING

LEVEL

Add a **B** to each of the words below and then rearrange the letters in each word to form a new seven-letter word.

E N C A S E

☐ ☐ ☐ ☐ ☐ ☐ ☐

H E R E A T

☐ ☐ ☐ ☐ ☐ ☐ ☐

T A H I N I

☐ ☐ ☐ ☐ ☐ ☐ ☐

R E N O W N

☐ ☐ ☐ ☐ ☐ ☐ ☐

Using any letters **EXCEPT** the ones that appear in the bunch below, fill in the blanks to form three new words.

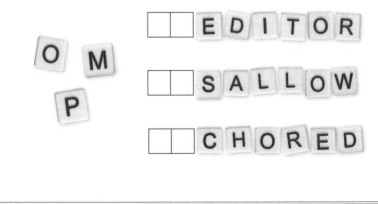

O M P

☐ ☐ E D I T O R

☐ ☐ S A L L O W

☐ ☐ C H O R E D

Using five of the tiles from each bunch on the left, fill in the blanks on the right to make an eight-letter word that connects the grid.

GO BANANAS!

LEVEL

Use all 21 tiles in this bunch to create a collection of connecting and intersecting common words in the grid below. **Any word that has more than two letters must be a sport.** The words may be horizontal or vertical, reading left to right or top to bottom.

LEVEL

Use all 21 tiles in this bunch to create a collection of connecting and intersecting common words in the grid below. **Each word must contain at least six letters.** The words may be horizontal or vertical, reading left to right or top to bottom.

BANANA BOATS

LEVEL

For each of the word groups below, change one letter in the top word to one of the letters that appears in the bottom word, then rearrange the tiles as needed to form a new common word. Do the same with each new word until you arrive at the bottom word. For example, one path from BARK to PLUM is BARK, MARK, RAMP, RUMP, PLUM.

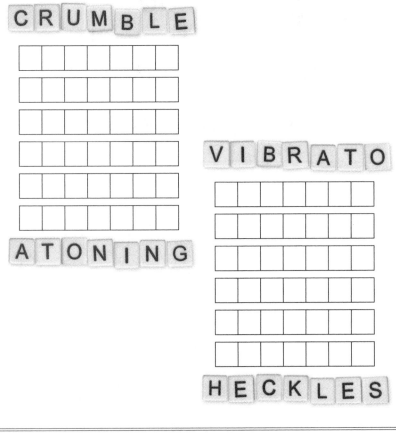

CRUMBLE

ATONING

VIBRATO

HECKLES

Each of the three-letter groups below may be extended both on the right and the left to form a nine-letter word. Drawing from the tiles directly above each group, fill in the blanks to find the words as quickly as you can.

A A C C N O Y

☐ ☐ ☐ D I D ☐ ☐ ☐

A C C E L R T

☐ ☐ ☐ H I T ☐ ☐ ☐

A C M N O T U

☐ ☐ ☐ B A T ☐ ☐ ☐

D E E G M R U

☐ ☐ ☐ A G O ☐ ☐ ☐

A I L P R T Y

☐ ☐ ☐ M I S ☐ ☐ ☐

BANANA SPLITS

For each of the three words below, change one letter to an R and then rearrange the letters to spell a type of animal.

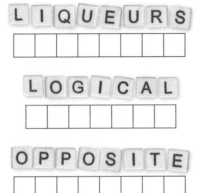

L I Q U E U R S

L O G I C A L

O P P O S I T E

For each of the three words below, change one letter to an A and then rearrange the letters to spell a type of food.

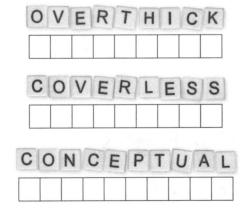

O V E R T H I C K

C O V E R L E S S

C O N C E P T U A L

238

Replace each of the question marks below with one of the vowels A, E, I, O or U **and then rearrange the letters to form a common word. Each vowel will be used only once.**

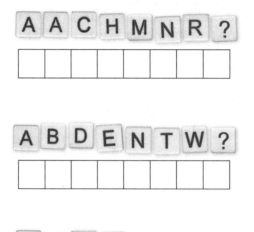

A A C H M N R ?

A B D E N T W ?

A D E H M O S ?

E F I L S T V ?

A C E H L O S ?

BANANA TREES

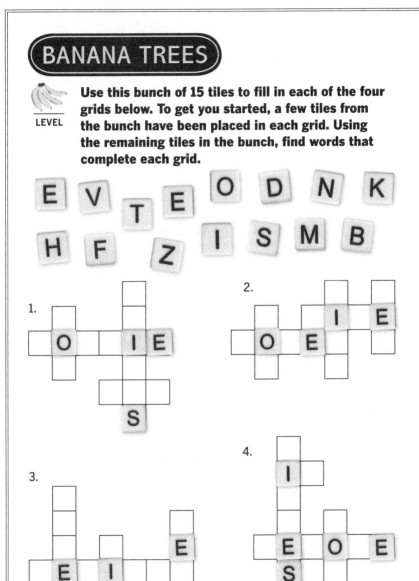

LEVEL

Use this bunch of 15 tiles to fill in each of the four grids below. To get you started, a few tiles from the bunch have been placed in each grid. Using the remaining tiles in the bunch, find words that complete each grid.

E V T E O D N K
H F Z I S M B

Use the 15 tiles in this bunch to create words that fit into the grids below. You will reuse this bunch for each of the four grids. The BANANA BITES provide hints to help you solve each grid.

A O E K H T W Z
E U G O J M V

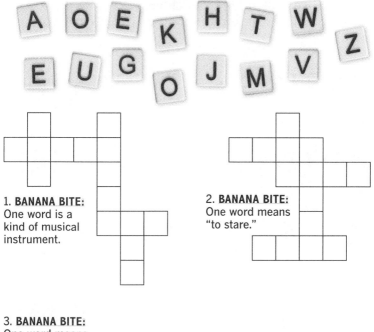

1. BANANA BITE:
One word is a kind of musical instrument.

2. BANANA BITE:
One word means "to stare."

3. BANANA BITE:
One word means "to declare openly."

4. BANANA BITE:
One word is a kind of puzzle.

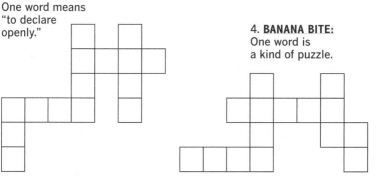

BANANA SHAKES

LEVEL

Each of the following seven-letter sets can be rearranged to spell out a common word that either starts with A, M or S and/or ends with E, G or L. How quickly can you find all the words?

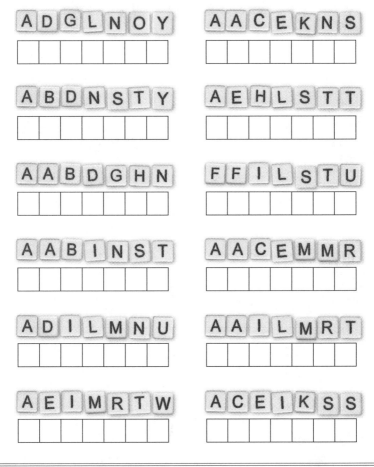

A D G L N O Y

A A C E K N S

A B D N S T Y

A E H L S T T

A A B D G H N

F F I L S T U

A A B I N S T

A A C E M M R

A D I L M N U

A A I L M R T

A E I M R T W

A C E I K S S

Each of the words below can be turned into another word on the list by changing one letter and then rearranging them all to form a new word. For example, REGIMENT can be turned into STEERING by changing the M to an S, so they would be a pair. How quickly can you find all the pairs?

Pairs

1. A L A B A S T E R

2. L E V I A T H A N _ _

3. O U T P R E A C H — —

4. A R T I C U L A R — —

5. R E H E A R S A L — —

6. D R A M A T I S T — —

7. S H A R E W A R E

8. A M P E R S A N D

9. A C T U A R I A L

10. P A R A C H U T E

11. M E T A T A R S I

12. S A N D P A P E R

13. B E T R A Y A L S

14. A L L E V I A N T

Using the 15 tiles in the bunch, fill in the spaces below according to the directions given.

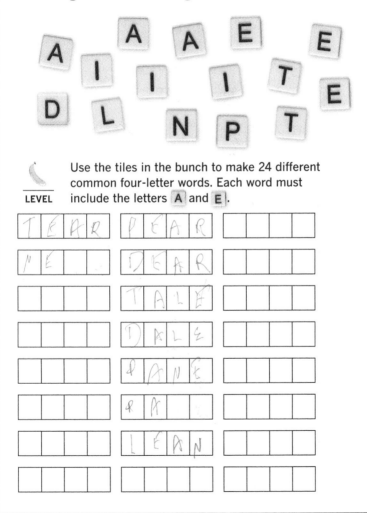

LEVEL

Use the tiles in the bunch to make 24 different common four-letter words. Each word must include the letters A and E.

T	E	A	R

P	E	A	R

N	E		

D	E	A	R

T	A	L	E

D	A	L	E

P	A	N	E

P	A		

L	E	A	N

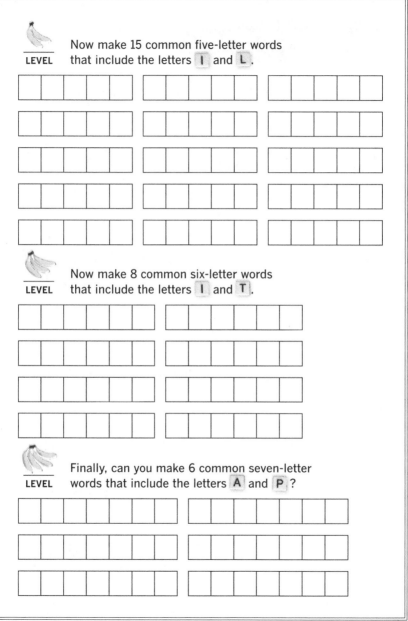

LEVEL Now make 15 common five-letter words that include the letters **I** and **L**.

LEVEL Now make 8 common six-letter words that include the letters **I** and **T**.

LEVEL Finally, can you make 6 common seven-letter words that include the letters **A** and **P**?

Add an H **to each of the words below and then rearrange the letters in each word to form a new seven-letter word.**

A L A R M S

☐☐☐☐☐☐☐

F E U D A L

☐☐☐☐☐☐☐

G A M I N G

☐☐☐☐☐☐☐

F E I N T S

☐☐☐☐☐☐☐

Using any letters EXCEPT the ones that appear in the bunch below, fill in the blanks to form three new words.

B E

N

☐☐ E D I B L E

☐☐ S T R I C T

☐☐ I N L A N D

246

Using five of the tiles from each bunch on the left, fill in the blanks on the right to make an eight-letter word that connects the grid.

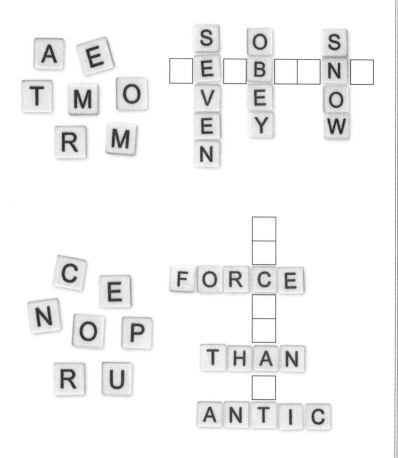

BANANA BOATS

LEVEL

For each of the word groups below, change one letter in the top word to one of the letters that appears in the bottom word, then rearrange the tiles as needed to form a new common word. Do the same with each new word until you arrive at the bottom word. For example, one path from **BARK** to **PLUM** is BARK, MARK, RAMP, RUMP, PLUM.

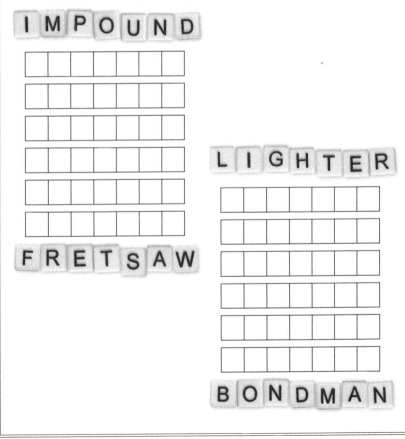

I M P O U N D

F R E T S A W

L I G H T E R

B O N D M A N

Each of the three-letter groups below may be extended both on the right and the left to form a nine-letter word. Drawing from the tiles directly above each group, fill in the blanks to find the words as quickly as you can.

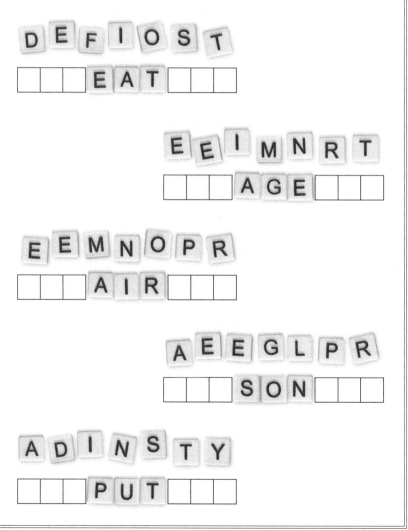

D E F I O S T

□ □ □ E A T □ □ □

E E I M N R T

□ □ □ A G E □ □ □

E E M N O P R

□ □ □ A I R □ □ □

A E E G L P R

□ □ □ S O N □ □ □

A D I N S T Y

□ □ □ P U T □ □ □

BANANA SPLITS

LEVEL

For each of the three words below, change one letter to a D and then rearrange the letters to spell a type of flower.

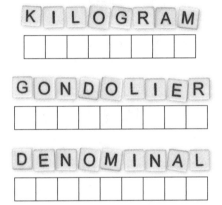

K I L O G R A M

G O N D O L I E R

D E N O M I N A L

For each of the three words below, change one letter to an R and then rearrange the letters to spell a color.

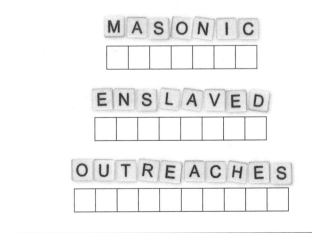

M A S O N I C

E N S L A V E D

O U T R E A C H E S

Replace each of the question marks below with one of the vowels A, E, I, O **or** U **and then rearrange the letters to form a common word. Each vowel will be used only once.**

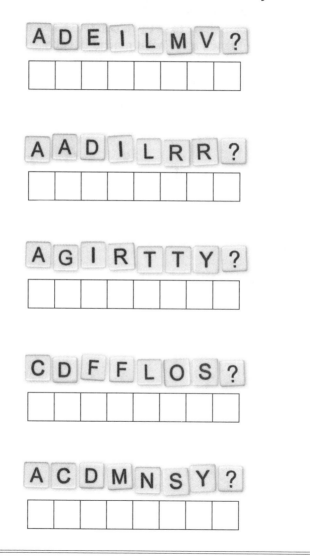

A D E I L M V ?

A A D I L R R ?

A G I R T T Y ?

C D F F L O S ?

A C D M N S Y ?

LEVEL

Use this bunch of 15 tiles to fill in each of the four grids below. To get you started, a few tiles from the bunch have been placed in each grid. Using the remaining tiles in the bunch, find words that complete each grid.

C B T E L E I T
U E D Z A R E

1.

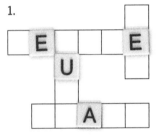

2.

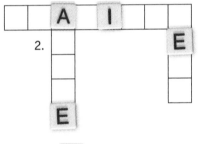

3.

4.

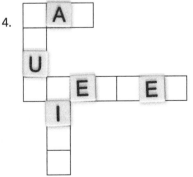

LEVEL

Use the 15 tiles in this bunch to create words that fit into the grids below. You will reuse this bunch for each of the four grids. The BANANA BITES provide hints to help you solve each grid.

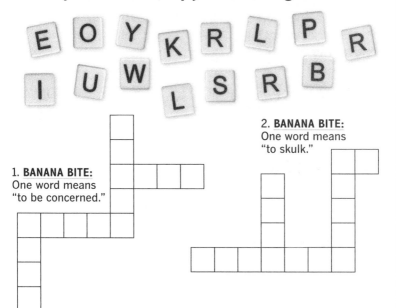

E O Y K R L P R
I U W L S R B

1. BANANA BITE:
One word means "to be concerned."

2. BANANA BITE:
One word means "to skulk."

3. BANANA BITE:
One word means "visually unclear."

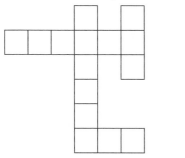

4. BANANA BITE:
One word is a kind of pack animal.

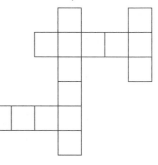

LEVEL

Each of the following seven-letter sets can be rearranged to spell out a common word that either starts with F, N or R and/or ends with E, N or Y. How quickly can you find all the words?

A C C F I L Y

B C H I M O R

E F N O R T U

C E E I K N T

A B I L R R Y

N N O O P R U

E E R S T T U

E E I M N S S

A D E G G R Y

A M N N O S W

A A E F F N R

D E G I L U V

254

Each of the words below can be turned into another word on the list by changing one letter and then rearranging them all to form a new word. For example, REGIMENT can be turned into STEERING by changing the M to an S, so they would be a pair. How quickly can you find all the pairs?

Pairs

1. HANDLEBAR

___ ___

2. ASSOCIATE

___ ___

3. STABLEMAN

___ ___

4. ANECDOTAL

___ ___

5. APPLECART

___ ___

6. OSTRACISE

___ ___

7. HEARTLAND

8. DEATHTRAP

9. COASTLAND

10. GUACAMOLE

11. APARTHEID

12. BEANSTALK

13. CATALOGUE

14. CATNAPPER

BANANA LEAVES

Using the 15 tiles in the bunch, fill in the spaces below according to the directions given.

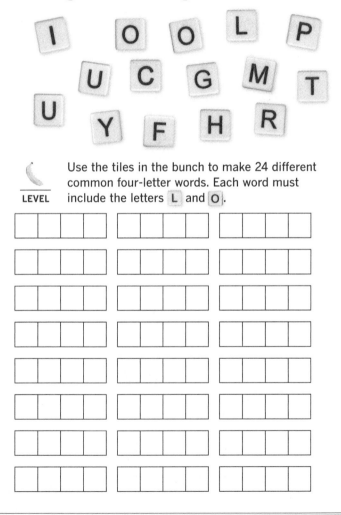

LEVEL

Use the tiles in the bunch to make 24 different common four-letter words. Each word must include the letters L and O.

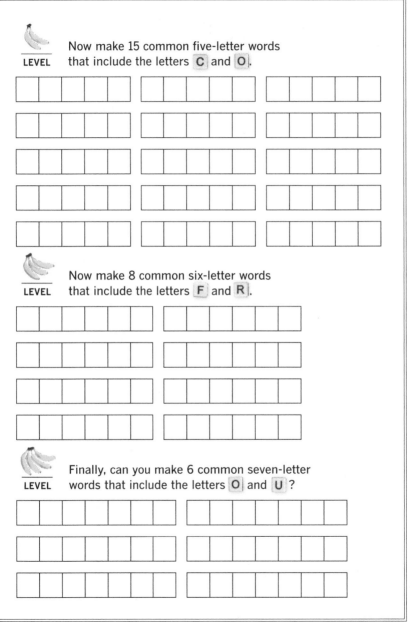

LEVEL Now make 15 common five-letter words that include the letters C and O.

LEVEL Now make 8 common six-letter words that include the letters F and R.

LEVEL Finally, can you make 6 common seven-letter words that include the letters O and U?

BANANA FILLING

LEVEL

Add a C **to each of the words below and then rearrange the letters in each word to form a new seven-letter word.**

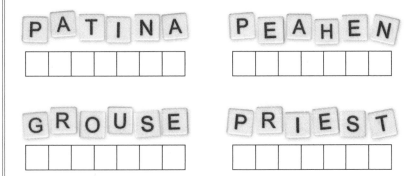

P A T I N A

P E A H E N

G R O U S E

P R I E S T

Using any letters EXCEPT the ones that appear in the bunch below, fill in the blanks to form three new words.

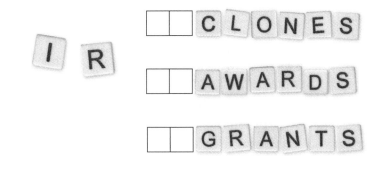

I R

C L O N E S

A W A R D S

G R A N T S

Using five of the tiles from each bunch on the left, fill in the blanks on the right to make an eight-letter word that connects the grid.

LEVEL

For each of the word groups below, change one letter in the top word to one of the letters that appears in the bottom word, then rearrange the tiles as needed to form a new common word. Do the same with each new word until you arrive at the bottom word. For example, one path from **BARK** to **PLUM** is **BARK, MARK, RAMP, RUMP, PLUM**.

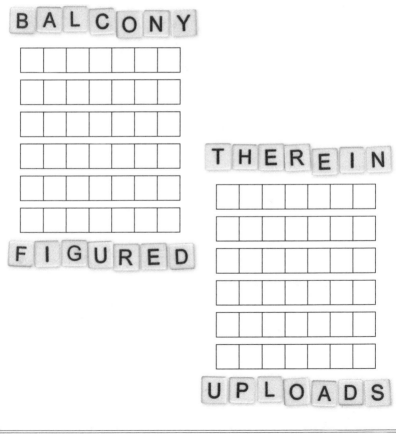

B A L C O N Y

F I G U R E D

T H E R E I N

U P L O A D S

Each of the three-letter groups below may be extended both on the right and the left to form a nine-letter word. Drawing from the tiles directly above each group, fill in the blanks to find the words as quickly as you can.

A A B E L M P

☐ ☐ ☐ T I S ☐ ☐ ☐

A C E I I N S

☐ ☐ ☐ V E T ☐ ☐ ☐

A D E I S T T

☐ ☐ ☐ E L L ☐ ☐ ☐

B N O R S U W

☐ ☐ ☐ G A L ☐ ☐ ☐

A C C E I N S

☐ ☐ ☐ R I F ☐ ☐ ☐

BANANA SPLITS

For each of the three words below, change one letter to a **T** and then rearrange the letters to spell a type of animal.

M A R C H E S

☐ ☐ ☐ ☐ ☐ ☐ ☐

S H A R P E N

☐ ☐ ☐ ☐ ☐ ☐ ☐

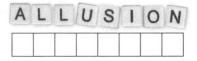

A L L U S I O N

☐ ☐ ☐ ☐ ☐ ☐ ☐ ☐

For each of the three words below, change one letter to an **R** and then rearrange the letters to spell a part of the body.

S I L I C O N

☐ ☐ ☐ ☐ ☐ ☐ ☐

B E E F A L O

☐ ☐ ☐ ☐ ☐ ☐ ☐

S A U C E P A N

☐ ☐ ☐ ☐ ☐ ☐ ☐ ☐

Replace each of the question marks below with one of the vowels A, E, I, O or U and then rearrange the letters to form a common word. Each vowel will be used only once.

E G I L O P S ?

A E I L N S Y ?

A A C L N P Y ?

A A A M N P R ?

A D G H L T Y ?

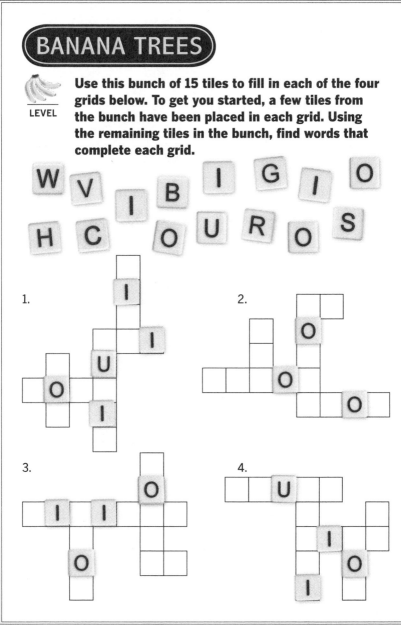

BANANA TREES

LEVEL

Use this bunch of 15 tiles to fill in each of the four grids below. To get you started, a few tiles from the bunch have been placed in each grid. Using the remaining tiles in the bunch, find words that complete each grid.

W V I B I G I O
H C O U R O S

1.

2.

3.

4.

LEVEL

Use the 15 tiles in this bunch to create words that fit into the grids below. You will reuse this bunch for each of the four grids. The BANANA BITES provide hints to help you solve each grid.

H E R J L A R E

C G A I T E I

2. BANANA BITE:
One word is a person who works in a school.

1. BANANA BITE:
One word means "wealthy."

3. BANANA BITE:
One word is a place you can find a lot of criminals.

4. BANANA BITE:
One word is a number.

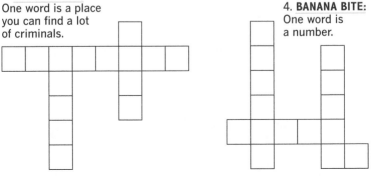

BANANA SHAKES

LEVEL

Each of the following seven-letter sets can be rearranged to spell out a common word that either starts with H **,** T **or** W **and/or ends with** C **,** M **or** S **. How quickly can you find all the words?**

C C H I N O R

D D E G O S S

D E H I O T U

I M O O S S S

A I N R S T T

E I M N O S W

M M O P S T Y

E E G H I N Y

A C I I R S T

E E F H O R W

A E E P R T Z

D G I K M N O

266

Each of the words below can be turned into another word on the list by changing one letter and then rearranging them all to form a new word. For example, REGIMENT can be turned into STEERING by changing the M to an S, so they would be a pair. How quickly can you find all the pairs?

Pairs

1. GALVANISE

2. ROUGHCAST   ___ ___

3. MAKEREADY   ___ ___

4. BAGATELLE   ___ ___

5. LANDSCAPE   ___ ___

6. ALTERABLE   ___ ___

7. PLEASANCE   ___ ___

8. SUGARCOAT

9. STAIRCASE

10. EARMARKED

11. ARCHANGEL

12. AVIATRESS

13. NAVIGABLE

14. FLAGRANCE

ANSWER KEY

PAGES 10–11

Possible solutions:

(Grid 1)
```
                        W
                        E
            Z           D
            E   S U R G E
        D   S T
      J E S T
    F U N   Y
      G
```

(Grid 2)
```
      W       Y
    G E E Z E R S
      N           U
      D       J A G
                  G
                F E U D
                  S
                  T
```

(Grid 3)
```
            J
    F       G A Z E D
    E           G
    W R U N G
                E
            D O U S E S
                      T
                      Y
```

PAGE 12

ARCH, CARD, DARN, DANK, KIND

ZINC, NICE, LINE, FILE, FLEW

BLOT, BOAT, COAT, CHAT, CHAP

PAGE 13

AFLOAT, DEPICT, FUTILE, REASON, DEFACE

PAGE 14

GOAT, LION, HORSE

FACE, CALF, FOOT

PAGE 15

SUDSY, ALIAS, RADII, COOED, NOBLY

PAGE 16

1.
```
    J           V
  T A W N Y     I
    W       E V E
    F U N
```

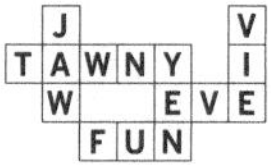

2.
```
          J
      V I E W
          V
      W E
      A
  F U N N Y
          T
```

3.
```
            W
            A
      W     V
  U N I F Y
      V
      J E T
          E
          N
```

4.
```
      W       I V Y
  J A U N T     E
      V         N
  F E W
```

PAGE 17

1.
```
          A
          V A T
          O
  P       I
  L U N G E D
  R
  E
```

2.
```
      P   A R E A
  V O L T
      N
  G U I D E
```

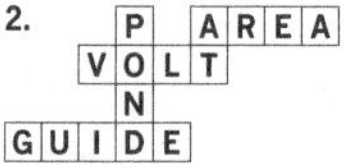

3.
```
            T
            A
  D R I V E N
      U       G
      L       O
  A P E
```

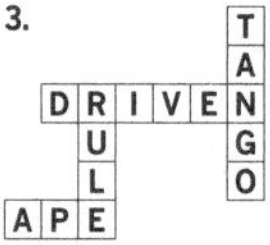

4.
```
        R
  G L O V E
        U
  P A I N T
  E     D
  A
```

PAGE 18

ROTATE, BETRAY, ENDURE, ETHNIC, MOSAIC, ENGINE, BECOME, FLUENT, LENGTH, WARMTH, FLAVOR, REFUTE

PAGE 19

1-6, 2-10, 3-9, 4-13, 5-7, 8-11, 12-14

PAGES 20–21

Possible solutions:

4-Letter Words:
MAUL, LUNA, LUAU, PUMA, AUNT, TUNA, AUTO, GULF, FOUL, TOFU, GLUM, LUNG, GULP, PLUG, GLUT, GOUT, LUMP, PLUM, LOUT, PULP, PUMP, UPON, PUNT, UNTO

5-Letter Words:
OMEGA, ALONE, ATONE, ALOFT, FLOAT, AFOUL, ALONG, GLOAT, AMONG, MANGO, TANGO, TALON, FELON, OFTEN, GLOVE

6-Letter Words:
MANUAL, PLAGUE, OUTAGE, AMULET, UNTAME, PEANUT, FLAUNT, MUTUAL

7-Letter Words:
OATMEAL, TANGELO, VOLTAGE, MONTAGE, UNGLOVE, OPULENT

PAGE 22

SALAD, ARGUE, CHAFE, NAIVE

GARAGE, ADRIFT, CUTOUT

PAGE 23

FACADE, GAMBIT

PAGES 24–25

Possible solutions:

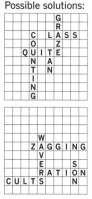

(Grid 1)
```
                G
                R
      C   L A S S
      O   Z
    Q U I T E
      N   A
      T   N
      I
      N
      G
```

(Grid 2)
```
      W
      Z A G G I N G
      V
      E         S
      R A T I O N
  C U L T S       N
```

PAGE 26

JAMB, BEAM, MACE, CAVE, VICE

DOOR, PROD, POUR, UPON, PUNY

HYMN, MANY, MOAN, ATOM, IOTA

PAGE 27

CASHEW, FLASHY, GAMINE, FEMALE, TUREEN

268

NEON, TIN, ARGON

PESO, EURO, POUND

BANJO, UNDID, THUMB, DEICE, HAZEL

1.

```
          W   F
    P A G E   E
        I     T
    D A T E S
```

2.

```
      W
  S T I F F
  P A D   E
  A G E   E
  T
```

3.
```
  S A F E
  W       A P E
  F I T T E D
  G
```

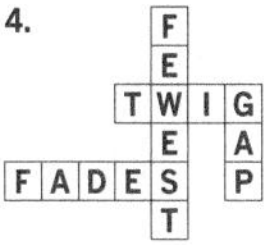

4.
```
        F
        E
      T W I G
      E     A
  F A D E S   P
      T
```

1.

```
    D O L L Y
    O
  C O N D O R
    O
    S O
```

2.
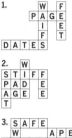
```
    D
    O
    O
  C O R N Y
  O
  L
  D
  S O L O
```

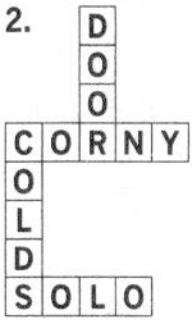

3.

```
        D
        O
  C O L O N Y
        O
        R
        S O L D
              O
```

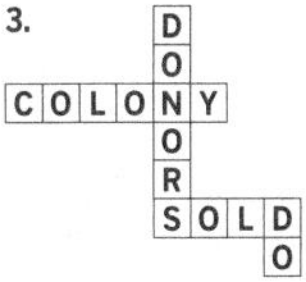

4.

```
  C
  O
  O
  L O O N Y
    D
    O
  L O R D S
```

STANZA, INSULT, RIBBON, STOLID, TENDON, MUTANT, HEMMED, CHANGE, CHOOSE, GASSED, CEMENT, INDUCE

1-8, 2-12, 3-6, 4-5, 7-9, 10-14, 11-13

Possible solutions:

4-Letter Words:
GALA, GLAD, DANG, GOAD, DRAG, GRAD, HANG, GOAL, RANG, GNAT, TANG, GOAT, TOGA, GOLD, DUNG, GOOD, DRUG, HUNG, THUG, LONG, LUNG, LOGO, GLUT, GOON

5-Letter Words:
KARAT, ALTAR, AURAL, AORTA, GRAND, GUARD, HOARD, DRANK, ADORN, GNARL, GROAN, ORGAN, GRANT, AUGUR, TAROT

6-Letter Words:
UNLOAD, AROUND, TUNDRA, NAUGHT, NOUGAT, OUTRAN, TRUANT, GROUND

7-Letter Words:
GARLAND, GRADUAL, GRANOLA, ANGULAR, GONDOLA, HANGOUT

IGLOO, BASIN, PATIO, RAINY

RADISH, TABOOS, THRUST

MALICE, FIASCO

Possible solutions:

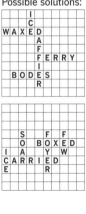
```
        I
        C
  W A X E D
        A
        F
        F E R R Y
        I
    B O D E S
        R
```

```
      S     F   F
      O   B O X E D
  I   A     Y   W
  C A R R I E D
  E       R
```

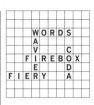
```
      W O R D S
      A
      V       C
    F I R E B O X
      E       D
  F I E R Y   A
```

HELP, PELT, TEMP, TIME, MITT

RUNT, TUNA, WANT, YAWN, WAVY

CHIN, NICE, REIN, PIER, PREY

GROWTH, BOUNTY, HEARSE, REHIRE, TRITON

HEEL, EYE, KIDNEY

ASP, SNAKE, COBRA

BEGUN, TWICE, GUMBO, LOGIC, EVADE

1.
```
  B R A I N Y
  O         E
  O         A
  E         R
  D O E
```

2.
```
  I O N
      E
      A
      R   R E A D
  O B O E
      Y
```

3.
```
              E
              A
          B A R E
  I R O N Y
  O
  D
  E
  O
```

4.

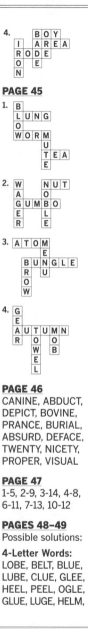

```
    B O Y
I   A R E A
R O D E
O   E
N
```

PAGE 45

1.
```
B
L U N G
O
W O R M
    U
    T E A
    E
```

2.
```
W       N U T
A       O
G U M B O
E       L
R       E
```

3.
```
A T O M
    E
  B U N G L E
  R   U
  O
  W
```

4.
```
G
E
A U T U M N
R   O   O
    W   B
    E
    L
```

PAGE 46
CANINE, ABDUCT, DEPICT, BOVINE, PRANCE, BURIAL, ABSURD, DEFACE, TWENTY, NICETY, PROPER, VISUAL

PAGE 47
1-5, 2-9, 3-14, 4-8, 6-11, 7-13, 10-12

PAGES 48–49
Possible solutions:

4-Letter Words:
LOBE, BELT, BLUE, LUBE, CLUE, GLEE, HEEL, PEEL, OGLE, GLUE, LUGE, HELM, HOLE, HELP, MOLE, MELT, MULE, OLEO, LOPE, POLE, LEPT, PELT, YELP, LUTE

5-Letter Words:
BOTCH, THUMB, BOOTH, CHUTE, CLOTH, COUTH, TOUCH, THEME, HOTEL, THYME, OUGHT, TOUGH, MOUTH, THUMP, PHOTO

6-Letter Words:
HUMBLE, CLOTHE, TOUCHE, HELMET, PHLEGM, HUGELY, HOMELY, PHOOEY

7-Letter Words:
BOOTLEG, COMPETE, COUPLET, OCTUPLE, COMMUTE, OUTCOME

PAGE 50
TROUT, SCOUT, URBAN, WOUND

GALORE, POLICE, KIMONO

PAGE 51
INVADE, HAIRDO

PAGES 52–53
Possible solutions:

```
            E
            L     H
            A     E
            T U X
            I
            O
        A   A N
        U   Y
    U N T I E
        O
```

```
          L
          E
          A
      A U N T   Y
      U       H E
    A U D I T I O N
      I       N
      O       E
```

PAGE 54
ORYX, YOUR, RUBY, CURB, CLUB

INTO, LION, LAIN, MAIL, ALUM

WAVE, ANEW, MEAN, MENU, NUMB

PAGE 55
CANOPY, SPINAL, OPENLY, SCREAM, HEREBY

PAGE 56
RAINY, SNOWY, STORMY

VOICE, SOUND, TENOR

PAGE 57
AFOOT, HUMID, CUTIE, PATIO, CABIN

PAGE 58

1.
```
      T
  F I E L D
      E
G     T
E     H
M E E T
```

2.
```
    F       T
    E       H
    T       E
    I       M
L E D G E
E
T
```

3.
```
        G
    D     I T
    E     F
H E L M E T
    E
    T
    E
```

4.
```
    T
    E
T H E F T
    M I
    L E
    E
  E D G E
```

PAGE 59

1.
```
          W
          A
F A L T E R
          B
          L
    D O Z E N
```

2.
```
        F
        E
    L   W A L T Z
B O N E   R
    A     R
    D
```

3.
```
F
O       W
B L A Z E R
A D     N
L       T
E
```

4.
```
              N
        F A L L O W
Z E B R A     T
              E
              D
```

PAGE 60
LAWMAN, MIDWAY, COLUMN, BEMOAN, ASTRAY, COPIED, MINNOW, THEORY, CONFER, THESIS, HUNTER, COZIER

PAGE 61
1-7, 2-12, 3-13, 4-11, 5-9, 6-8, 10-14

PAGES 62–63

Possible solutions:

4-Letter Words:
CALM, CLAM, COMA, CAMP, LOAM, CRAM, HARM, MATH, LIMA, MAIL, MAIN, LAMP, PALM, MALT, MAUL, MOAN, MANY, ROAM, ATOM, MOAT, MAYO, RAMP, PUMA, TRAM

5-Letter Words:
ALARM, ALTAR, AURAL, LARCH, CAROL, CORAL, TRAIL, TRIAL, MOLAR, MORAL, MURAL, LUNAR, POLAR, ROYAL, LURCH

6-Letter Words:
PAUNCH, UTOPIA, PUNCHY, UNCLIP, TURNIP, PURITY, PUNILY, PAYOUT

7-Letter Words:
CHARIOT, MONARCH, PHANTOM, HARMONY, ATROPHY, MONTHLY

PAGE 64

PEEVE, LOOSE, FLEET, LATHE

INTONE, ENVIED, ERMINE

PAGE 65

WEAPON, NAUGHT

PAGES 66–67

Possible solutions:

PAGE 68

MINI, MAIN, NAIL, LAWN, WALK

DODO, DOOR, ROAD, DARE, REAR

WHEW, PHEW, HEAP, PAVE, VAMP

PAGE 69

ENMESH, STUPOR, SHADOW, EYEFUL, GEISHA

PAGE 70

PLUM, PICKLE, APPLE

TOOTH, MOUTH, HEART

PAGE 71

VOCAB, BOGUS, FORCE, ETUDE, AUDIT

PAGE 72

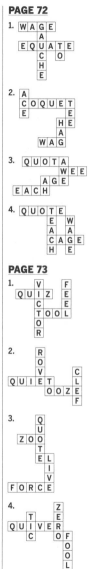

1. WAGE / EQUATE / C O / H / E

2. A / COQUET / E / E / HE / A / WAG

3. QUOTA / WEE / AGE / EACH

4. QUOTE / E W / A A / CAGE / H E

PAGE 73

1. V F / QUIZ E / C E / TOOL / O / R

2. R / O / V C / QUIET L / OOZE / F

3. Q / U / ZOO / T / EL / I / V / FORCE

4. Z / T E / QUIVER / C OF / O / O / L

PAGE 74

TWELVE, CLAMOR, FAUCET, SHOULD, BASKET, DOCTOR, BESTOW, SHADOW, TWITCH, REWIRE, REVOLT, INFLOW

PAGE 75

1-6, 2-9, 3-7, 4-12, 5-13, 8-11, 10-14

PAGES 76–77

Possible solutions:

4-Letter Words:
DEER, REED, DIRE, IRED, RIDE, NERD, REND, RUDE, RUED, LEER, REEL, PEER, TREE, RILE, REIN, PIER, RIPE, RITE, TIER, TIRE, LURE, RULE, RENT, PURE

5-Letter Words:
LINED, PINED, DINER, TINED, LINER, INLET, RIPEN, INEPT, INERT, URINE, UNITE, UNTIE, UNLIT, UNTIL, PINUP

6-Letter Words:
NEEDLE, LENDER, RELENT, RELINE, UNREEL, NETTLE, NIPPLE, LINEUP

7-Letter Words:
DEPLETE, PRETEND, ERUPTED, REPUTED, TRIPLED, PRINTED

PAGE 78

ROACH, OWNER, TROOP, TABOO

ACCORD, VACANT, UNSUNG

PAGE 79
EMBLEM, GOTHIC

PAGES 80–81
Possible solutions:

PAGE 82
PLANT, PLATE, ALTER, ORATE, ADORE, RODEO

RAPID, DRAPE, PAGER, GRAVE, VAGUE, VOGUE

FOCAL, CORAL, CAROB, BARON, BRAIN, BRINE

PAGE 83
ADVANCE, MILITIA, CARIBOU, CABINET, ANTONYM

PAGE 84
FOUL, LAYUP, GUARD

PANDA, FINCH, HYENA

PAGE 85
SASHAY, BANDIT, UNCLOG, ACUMEN, TOUCHÉ

PAGE 86

1.
```
Y
I
E X P O R T
L       U
D I O D E
```

2.
```
E X I L E D
          R
          O
          O
          P I
    D U T Y
```

3.
```
P
O
O     D U E
D     I
L     R
E X I T
      Y
```

4.
```
D E T O U R
I   D
D   L
    E P O X Y
```

PAGE 87

1.
```
          A
          G
      M A T E
          I
H E A V E N
      D
      D
```

2.
```
              D
              E
              E
H   M A I D
V E G A N
A
T
```

3.
```
        N
H I V E E
D     G
E     A
A     T
      E
M A D
```

4.
```
M E D I A
A       H A V E N
D
G E T
```

PAGE 88
INSULTS, RETIREE, RETITLE, PAGEANT, RIOTOUS, INSTANT, UNSTRAP, WACKIER, UNSNARL, RAMPANT, HEAVIER, OBVIOUS

PAGE 89
1-6, 2-8, 3-10, 4-14, 5-11, 7-13, 9-12

PAGES 90–91
Possible solutions:

4-Letter Words:
BORN, BOOR, CORD, CORN, CROP, LORD, DOOR, ODOR, DROP, PROD, TROD, IRON, RIOT, TRIO, ROLL, TORN, POOR, ROOT, PORT, ROPY, TYRO, ROIL, DORY, TORY

5-Letter Words:
BROIL, ROBIN, ORBIT, IONIC, TONIC, OPTIC, TOPIC, IDIOT, DOILY, POLIO, PILOT, PINTO, POINT, INTRO, IRONY

6-Letter Words:
DOCTOR, NITRIC, TROPIC, TOROID, TRIPOD, PORTLY, PRONTO, PROTON

7-Letter Words:
BICOLOR, IDYLLIC, BLINDLY, BILLION, POLITIC, COPILOT

PAGE 92
DENTAL, TAVERN, NORMAL, DONKEY

ANOTHER, AWFULLY, WASTAGE

PAGE 93
PROVERB, MELODIC

PAGES 94–95
Possible solutions:

PAGE 96

TOUCH, CHUTE, ACUTE, CLEAT, VALET, ALIVE

GLYPH, LYMPH, IMPLY, IMPEL, PRIME, MERIT

UNDID, DINED, DINER, BRIDE, BORED, PROBE

PAGE 97

DARESAY, ERRATIC, HYGIENE, INHERIT, ROMANCE

PAGE 98

PRUNE, PECAN, WALNUT

TUNA, TROUT, SMELT

PAGE 99

LETHAL, IGUANA, DAMPEN, ABOUND, BENIGN

PAGE 100

1.

```
  K       A
  N       U
N A I V E R
  T       A
        S E E
```

2.

```
S
E
V A I N
E
N U K E
    A
    R
    A
    T
```

3.

```
  V I S A
N       U
E A T E N
A       K
R E
```

4.

```
R E T I N A S
  A
A V E N U E
  K
```

PAGE 101

1.

```
        T E E
    G O
    O
I   O
C H A F E
E   Y
```

2.

```
    C
  G O O E Y
    O   H E
F E A T
    I
    E
```

3.

```
E     H O O F
Y O G I     E
E           E
      C A T
```

4.

```
C O Y O T E
H       O
I       G
E       A
F E E
```

PAGE 102

DROUGHT, UPTIGHT, COMPETE, BASHFUL, TRIVIAL, SUBHEAD, REFUSER, TRINITY, COARSER, GLEEFUL, COMMEND, SUBSIDE

PAGE 103

1-5, 2-9, 3-11, 4-7, 6-14, 8-13, 10-12

PAGES 104–105

Possible solutions:

4-Letter Words:
LACE, COAL, COLA, CLAP, TALC, CLAW, CLAY, LACY, HALE, HEAL, LEAP, PALE, PEAL, PLEA, EARL, REAL, LATE, TALE, VEAL, HALO, HALT, HAUL, HULA, OPAL

5-Letter Words:
COACH, POACH, ROACH, HAVOC, CAROL, CORAL, VOCAL, ACTOR, COUCH, OCCUR, EPOCH, CHORE, CLOVE, COVER, COWER

6-Letter Words:
ALCOVE, OCTAVE, CAVORT, CLOVER, VELCRO, COVERT, VECTOR, REVOLT

7-Letter Words:
CHEAPLY, OVERLAP, OUTPLAY, COUPLET, OCTUPLE, POULTRY

PAGE 106

BRUTAL, COWARD, CALICO, LOCALE

THREADS, RADIALS, PLAGUES

PAGE 107

BOOKLET, BULLPEN

PAGES 108–109

Possible solutions:

```
    B
V A G U E
I   M
A   P A
    C         F
    U         U
    T O W E R
    E
```

```
        C
      A F O O T
B R O O M   P   U
E           A G E
A           W
U       V I E
```

PAGE 110

PHONE, HOPED, PORED, PRIDE, AIRED, RADII

VIDEO, LIVED, ALIVE, VIRAL, LARVA, ALARM

COMMA, CAMEO, OMEGA, IMAGE, AGILE, GUILE

PAGE 111

DIALECT, EMBARGO, HALIBUT, JOURNAL, RELIEVE

PAGE 112

VIOLIN, PIANO, GUITAR

CEDAR, SPRUCE, CHERRY

PAGE 113

BURLAP, NICETY, SOAKED, SONATA, ACTUAL

PAGE 114

1.
```
G
A T
V I D E O
E       A
        T A U T
        H
```

2.
```
E
I
G A T E D
H       A
T O U T
    V
    A
```

3.
```
    D
G E T
    V
    I   A H A
    A U T O
    T
    E
```

4.
```
    T       A
    H E A V E
    A     T O
G U T     I
        D
```

PAGE 115

1.
```
            S
            H
            U
        N I N N Y
S O O N
O
D
A
```

2.
```
    I
N O O N
O   N
U   S
N
S H A D Y
```

3.
```
        O
H A N D
O N   I
      O
      S U N N Y
      S
```

4.
```
        A
S O U N D S
    O O H
    N   I
        N
        N
        Y
```

PAGE 116
CAVEMAN, RETRACT, FIREMAN, HEADWAY, EMBASSY, FEATURE, HEADSET, GRAVEST, CULTURE, RETOTAL, EMBROIL, WARMEST

PAGE 117
1-9, 2-4, 3-10, 5-14, 6-12, 7-13, 8-11

PAGES 118–119
Possible solutions:

4-Letter Words:
LAVA, BAIL, BALL, BAWL, CALL, CLAN, COAL, COLA, CLAP, CLAW, LAIN, NAIL, PAIL, ALIT, TAIL, VIAL, WAIL, TALL, WALL, LOAN, PLAN, LAWN, ALTO, OVAL

5-Letter Words:
BANAL, CANAL, AVAIL, NAVAL, BLOAT, LILAC, LOCAL, VOCAL, VILLA, PLAIN, ANVIL, VIOLA, VITAL, ALLOT, ALLOW

6-Letter Words:
CANOLA, COBALT, OILCAN, ACTION, CATION, CALLOW, CANNOT, COWPAT

7-Letter Words:
COALBIN, BOTANIC, CANNOLI, CONTAIN, CAPTION, LANOLIN

PAGE 120
VANDAL, ELDEST, RADISH, DIVIDE

HISTORY, NEGATED, PREDICT

PAGE 121
CONFUSE, VEHICLE

PAGES 122–123
Possible solutions:

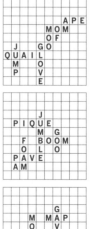

PAGE 124
COLOR, CORAL, CARGO, GRACE, RAGED, ADAGE

HORAH, ROACH, NACHO, OCEAN, CLEAN, UNCLE

GLEAM, AGILE, IDEAL, OILED, VIDEO, OVOID

PAGE 125
CRYONIC, DESPAIR, ALMANAC, MATADOR, HABITAT

PAGE 126
BARLEY, GRAPES, BURGER

ROBIN, PIGEON, SPARROW

PAGE 127
TABLED, AVOWAL, POUNCE, IMPACT, UNFAIR

PAGE 128

1.
```
            L
N O R       U
    U       G
    I N V O K E
    N
    Y
```

2.
```
Y O L K
    U
    N
    G O V E R N
          U
          I
          N
```

3.
```
Y
O
N U K I N G
O R     U
V       N
E
L
```

274

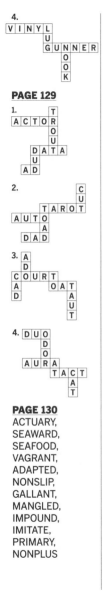

4.

V	I	N	Y	L
			U	
		G	U	N	N	E	R
			O	
			O	
			K	

PAGE 129

1.

```
        T
A C T O R
        O
        U
    D A T A
        U
    A D
```

2.

```
            C
            U
        T A R O T
A U T O       A
        D A D
```

3.

```
A
D
C O U R T
A       O A T
D       A
        U
        T
```

4.

```
D U O
    D
    O
A U R A
    T A C T
    A
    T
```

PAGE 130

ACTUARY,
SEAWARD,
SEAFOOD,
VAGRANT,
ADAPTED,
NONSLIP,
GALLANT,
MANGLED,
IMPOUND,
IMITATE,
PRIMARY,
NONPLUS

PAGE 131

1-7, 2-10, 3-14, 4-11,
5-9, 6-13, 8-12

PAGES 132–133
Possible solutions:

4-Letter Words:
BLOB, BLOC,
BOLD, BOIL,
CLOD, COLD,
COIL, LOCI,
CLOP, CLOY,
HOLD, IDOL,
MOLD, PLOD,
LORD, LOUD,
HOLY, LIMO,
LION, LOIN,
ROIL, OILY,
ONLY, PLOY

5-Letter Words:
BIRCH, CLIMB,
CHILD, CHIRP,
CHOIR, CHIMP,
CRIMP, CUMIN,
CUPID, LUCID,
LYRIC, INCUR,
CURIO, PRICY,
PINCH

6-Letter Words:
BODILY, MORBID,
DOUBLY, ORCHID,
CLOUDY, HOLDUP,
PODIUM, MOULDY

7-Letter Words:
BUBONIC,
INBOUND,
UNICORN,
IMPOUND,
ROUNDLY,
PURLOIN

PAGE 134

IMPORT, BIRDIE,
FUTILE, SPIRIT

SUSTAIN,
LABORER,
UPFIELD

PAGE 135

DEADPAN,
HUSBAND

PAGES 136–137
Possible solutions:

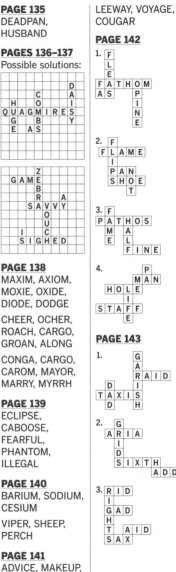

```
                    D
            C       A
    H       O       I
Q U A G M I R E S
    G       B       Y
    E       A S
```

```
            Z
    G A M E
            B
            R       A
        S A V V Y
            O
            U
        I   C
        S I G H E D
```

PAGE 138

MAXIM, AXIOM,
MOXIE, OXIDE,
DIODE, DODGE

CHEER, OCHER,
ROACH, CARGO,
GROAN, ALONG

CONGA, CARGO,
CAROM, MAYOR,
MARRY, MYRRH

PAGE 139

ECLIPSE,
CABOOSE,
FEARFUL,
PHANTOM,
ILLEGAL

PAGE 140

BARIUM, SODIUM,
CESIUM

VIPER, SHEEP,
PERCH

PAGE 141

ADVICE, MAKEUP,
LEEWAY, VOYAGE,
COUGAR

PAGE 142

1.

```
F
L
E
F A T H O M
A S       P
          I
          N
          E
```

2.

```
F
F L A M E
I
P A N
S H O E
    T
```

3.

```
F
P A T H O S
M       A
E       L
        F I N E
```

4.

```
            P
        M A N
H O L E
    I
S T A F F
    E
```

PAGE 143

1.

```
        G
        A
        R A I D
    D   I
T A X I S
    D   H
```

2.

```
    G
A R I A
    I
    D
    S I X T H
        A D D
```

3.

```
R I D
I
G A D
H
T   A I D
S A X
```

275

4.
```
D A T A
    A X
  H I D
R I G I D
    S
```

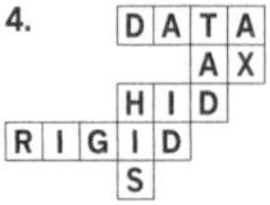

PAGE 144
EVIDENT, CATFISH, FOREIGN, OUTLEAP, FORESAW, RADIOED, SELFISH, CHEERIO, CONSENT, WATCHED, OUTWAIT, CHEAPEN

PAGE 145
1-12, 2-6, 3-9, 4-13, 5-10, 7-14, 8-11

PAGES 146–147
Possible solutions:

4-Letter Words:
AURA, CRAB, BOAR, BRAT, BRAY, CRAM, CARP, CRAP, CART, RACY, CZAR, ROAM, RAMP, MART, TRAM, ARMY, ROAR, PART, RAPT, TARP, TRAP, PRAY, ORCA, TRAY

5-Letter Words:
CARAT, AROMA, AORTA, APART, ARRAY, CAROB, COBRA, RUMBA, ARBOR, CAROM, CRAMP, CARRY, CRAZY, ARMOR, MAYOR

6-Letter Words:
TRAUMA, COMBAT, ABRUPT, CAPTOR, CARROT, MORTAR, PARROT, RAPTOR

7-Letter Words:
ACROBAT, ACTUARY, COMPACT, COPYCAT, CURATOR, CORRUPT

PAGE 148
GLAMOR, NEGATE, BUDGET, DELUGE

PREVENT, WASHOUT, TAMALES

PAGE 149
REDWOOD, FACTUAL

PAGE 150
```
        J E W E L
        Q
        U
    P E A C E
        T
        I
        O
  M A T I N G
```

PAGE 151
```
          R G
          H O
        G I R A F F E
          N T R
  H I P P O     O
                G
```

PAGE 152
TEABOX, BORATE, ATONER, NATURE, UNREAL, URINAL, RULING

FRIGID, FIRING, FINGER, REGAIN, RETINA, RENTAL, MANTLE

PAGE 153
AMBROSIA, GRANDSON, FILAMENT, INDUSTRY, COHERENT

PAGE 154
RADISH, PEANUT, SOYBEAN

MADRID, MUMBAI, MONTREAL

PAGE 155
EPISODE, REMNANT, HEARSAY, DIPLOMA, GRADUAL

PAGE 156
1. 
```
          D
        Y E
F R O N T
        N
        D
        E
        R A N T
```
2. 
```
T A N
  T         Y
F O R D E D
  N         N
  E
  R
```
3.
```
          A
          T
          T
F
O R N E R Y
N         N E
D         D
```

4.
```
F E N D
R
T Y R A N T
O
N
E
D
```

PAGE 157
1. 
```
    A
    W
    O       G
J O K E R
A     E     I
M           T
            S
```
2. 
```
              K
              I
              T A G
              E
M A J O R S
E
O
W
```
3. 
```
              W
        J     A
        O     G
M I S T A K E
        O
        R
        E
```
4.
```
              T
              I
              G
        M     E
        A J A R
        K
        E
W O O S
```

PAGE 158
OVERUSE, OVERDID, TESTIFY, BLATANT, FIGMENT, BOOKLET, OUTSWAM, STRIVER, SPECIFY, DROPLET, VARMINT, STROKED

1-3, 2-6, 4-13, 5-11, 7-9, 8-12, 10-14

PAGES 160–161

Possible solutions:

4-Letter Words:
IDLE, LIED, DIME, DINE, DIRE, IRED, RIDE, DIET, EDIT, TIDE, TIED, LIME, MILE, LINE, PILE, RILE, TILE, MIEN, MINE, EMIT, ITEM, MITE, TIME, REIN

5-Letter Words:
PILED, PLIED, PINED, PRIDE, PRIED, UPEND, PRUDE, IMPEL, PERIL, PLIER, PRIME, RIPEN, INEPT, RIPER, LETUP

6-Letter Words:
IMPEND, PRUNED, PUNTED, PUNDIT, LINEUP, PUNIER, UNRIPE, PUNTER

7-Letter Words:
LIMITED, TRILLED, TENDRIL, TRIPLED, TRUNDLE, LINTIER

PAGE 162

ARCANE, CATNIP, ACROSS, OCTANE

MASTIFFS, TOWELLED, PARENTAL

PAGE 163

VERDICT, WEEKEND

PAGE 164

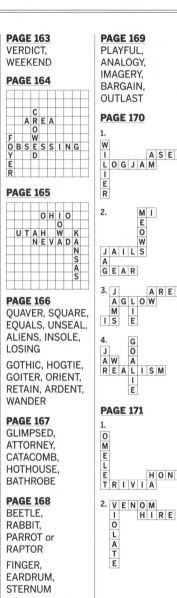

PAGE 165

PAGE 166

QUAVER, SQUARE, EQUALS, UNSEAL, ALIENS, INSOLE, LOSING

GOTHIC, HOGTIE, GOITER, ORIENT, RETAIN, ARDENT, WANDER

PAGE 167

GLIMPSED, ATTORNEY, CATACOMB, HOTHOUSE, BATHROBE

PAGE 168

BEETLE, RABBIT, PARROT or RAPTOR

FINGER, EARDRUM, STERNUM

PAGE 169

PLAYFUL, ANALOGY, IMAGERY, BARGAIN, OUTLAST

PAGE 170

1.

2.

3.

4.

PAGE 171

1.

2.

PAGE 172

MIDLINE, MIDYEAR, OUTTALK, ANDROID, ABSOLVE, TABLOID, OUTROOT, ABSCOND, CUISINE, IMAGINE, BUYABLE, PAYABLE

PAGE 173

1-4, 2-6, 3-10, 5-14, 7-12, 8-13, 9-11

PAGES 174–175

Possible solutions:

4-Letter Words:
BITE, DIET, EDIT, TIDE, TIED, DIRT, TILE, EMIT, ITEM, MITE, TIME, TINE, RITE, TIER, TIRE, GILT, GRIT, TWIG, HILT, HINT, THIN, WITH, WHIT, LINT

5-Letter Words:
BERTH, HEDGE, HEWED, HIRED,

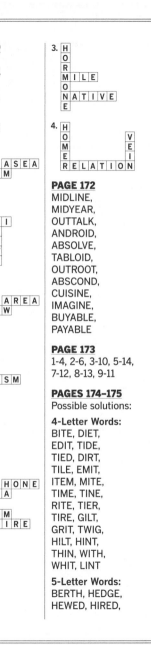

DEPTH, WHEEL, THEME, ETHER, THREE, THERE, WHERE, HINGE, EIGHT, WEIGH, WHILE

6-Letter Words:
WHILED, WHINED, WHITED, NEPHEW, HEWING, WEIGHT, WHITEN, WHITER

7-Letter Words:
BIRTHED, HUMBLED, THUMBED, THIMBLE, BLITHER, HUMBLER

PAGE 176
ONLINE, ONWARD, AFLOAT, COPIER

MALINGER, FEDERATE, INSANITY

PAGE 177
MANKIND, DIPLOMA

PAGE 178

PAGE 179
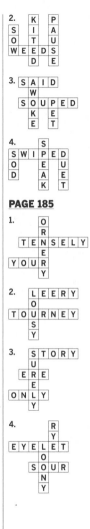

PAGE 180
PLAYER, NEARLY, LANDER, DENTAL, DETAIN, UNITED, INDUCT

TUMULT, MUTUAL, AMULET, HAMLET, LATHER, WREATH, WHARVE

PAGE 181
OBSOLETE, HOSPITAL, OILINESS, COLOSSAL, CAMISOLE

PAGE 182
DRESSER, ARMOIRE, RECLINER

TAYLOR, MONROE, MADISON

PAGE 183
CATALOG, CORDIAL, BANDAGE, PATIENT, LAWSUIT

PAGE 184

PAGE 185

PAGE 186
ABYSMAL, CANDIES, OVERBID, OVERSEE, ELUSIVE, RADICAL, REFRAIN, DAISIES, CONNIVE, UNPAVED, UNCHAIN, RENEWAL

PAGE 187
1-6, 2-11, 3-8, 4-14, 5-12, 7-10, 9-13

PAGES 188–189
Possible solutions:

4-Letter Words:
HELP, HEMP, HOPE, PHEW, HYPE, PILE, PIER, RIPE, WIPE, YIPE, LOPE, POLE, LEPT, PELT, YELP, MOPE, POEM, PERM, TEMP, PORE, ROPE, POET, PERT, PREY

5-Letter Words:
WEIGH, WHILE, WHITE, WHOLE, THREW, WIPER, WRITE, LOWER, TOWEL, WETLY, MOWER, WHELP, POWER, TOWER, WROTE

6-Letter Words:
PILFER, FILTER, TRIFLE, FLIGHT, FRIGHT, FIRMLY, PROFIT, TYPIFY

7-Letter Words:
WHIMPER,
IMPERIL,
WIMPIER,
IMPLORE,
POLYMER,
PILGRIM

PAGE 190
EITHER, ERSATZ,
GEYSER, GENIAL

ACCURATE,
BALANCES,
MISWORDS

PAGE 191
RANSACK,
BREADTH

PAGE 192

PAGE 192 grid:
```
        F
      A   A
      S   U
    Z T   T
    A E   O
E X P O N E N T S
      Y
```

PAGE 193

PAGE 193 grid:
```
  R A D I C A L S
              Q
              U
              I
              N
              T
  P R O J E C T S
```

PAGE 194
AIRWAY, WARILY,
WAILER, ÉCLAIR,
RECOIL, POLICE,
COUPLE

RADIUM, ADMIRE,
TIRADE, DETAIL,
TOILED, LOOTED,
OCELOT

PAGE 195
HEREINTO,

ARRANGED,
ENTANGLE,
KEROSENE,
LEGALESE

PAGE 196
ORCHID, HOLLY,
HYACINTH

TONGUE, THROAT,
STOMACH

PAGE 197
OREGANO,
ACROBAT,
PREVAIL,
MACHINE,
EARMUFF

PAGE 198

1.
```
S
O
I       M O U S E
L E V E R   E
            E
```

2.
```
S
I
E
V O L U M E S
E     E   O
      R
      E
```

3.
```
      E S S
M         E
O         E
V E L O U R
I
E
```

4.
```
L O U S I E R
            E
      S E E M
            O
            V
            E
```

PAGE 199

1.
```
E
N
E V A D E D
O       E
Y       B
        A
        T
        E
```

2.
```
        E
        B
D E V O T E E
A       N
D       Y E A
```

3.
```
          D
    D     A
    O B E Y
V A N E
  T E E
  E
```

4.
```
A D       E
    A B O V E
  D Y E     E
      E     N
            T
```

PAGE 200
UPSTAGE,
CALCIUM,
EXPANSE,
UPENDED,
NEATEST,
PRETEND,
DOGLIKE or
GODLIKE,
MADDEST,
PREMIUM,
WARLIKE,
PREVIEW,
EXACTLY

PAGE 201
1-9, 2-8, 3-12, 4-11,
5-14, 6-13, 7-10

PAGES 202–203
Possible solutions:

4-Letter Words:
DIAL, LAID,
FAIL, LIMA,
MAIL, PAIL,
LAIR, LIAR,
RAIL, ALIT,
TAIL, IDLE,
LIED, MILD,
FILE, LIFE,
LIME, MILE,
PILE, RILE,
TILE, FILM,

FLIP, LIFT

5-Letter Words:
FARED, DRAFT,
AFIRE, FERAL,
FLARE, FLAIR,
FRAIL, FIRED,
FRIED, DRIFT,
GRIEF, FLIER,
RIFLE, REFIT,
FLIRT

6-Letter Words:
TAMALE, PALATE,
LARIAT, DETAIL,
DILATE, TAILED,
RETAIL, FALTER

7-Letter Words:
DAMAGED,
DIAGRAM,
RAMPAGE,
MIGRATE,
RAGTIME,
GLIMMER

PAGE 204
FAUCET, FERVOR,
SAFARI, FIFTHS

MIGRATES,
OUTRANKS,
LIFELINE

PAGE 205
ASCETIC,
CYANIDE

PAGE 206

PAGE 206 grid:
```
  L
  O
  C
  K
P E N C I L
  R   H
      H A L L
          L
D E S K
```

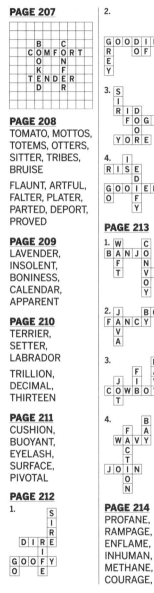

		B		C				
	C	O	M	F	O	R	T	
		O		N				
		K		F				
	T	E	N	D	E	R		
		D		R				

PAGE 208
TOMATO, MOTTOS, TOTEMS, OTTERS, SITTER, TRIBES, BRUISE

FLAUNT, ARTFUL, FALTER, PLATER, PARTED, DEPORT, PROVED

PAGE 209
LAVENDER, INSOLENT, BONINESS, CALENDAR, APPARENT

PAGE 210
TERRIER, SETTER, LABRADOR

TRILLION, DECIMAL, THIRTEEN

PAGE 211
CUSHION, BUOYANT, EYELASH, SURFACE, PIVOTAL

PAGE 212
1.

		S
		I
		R
D	I	R	E
		I
G	O	O	F	Y
O		E

2.

					I
					R
					I
G	O	O	D	I	E	S
R		O	F
E
Y

3.

S
I
R	I	D
	F	O	G	I	E
	O
Y	O	R	E

4.

	I
R	I	S	E
	D
G	O	O	I	E	R
O		F
	Y

PAGE 213
1.

W		C
B	A	N	J	O
	F		N
	T		V	I	A
			O
			Y

2.

J		B	O	O	T
F	A	N	C	Y		W
V					I
A					N

3.

			N
		F		A
J		I		V	A	N
C	O	W	B	O	Y
T

4.

		B
	F		A
W	A	V	Y
	C
	T
J	O	I	N
	O
	N

PAGE 214
PROFANE, RAMPAGE, ENFLAME, INHUMAN, METHANE, COURAGE, DISDAIN, DRASTIC, ENCRYPT, DISOBEY, INHIBIT, ARCHAIC

PAGE 215
1-14, 2-7, 3-11, 4-9, 5-12, 6-13, 8-10

PAGES 216–217
Possible solutions:

4-Letter Words:
BACK, CRAB, HACK, CHAP, ARCH, CHAR, CHAT, ACHY, LACK, PACK, RACK, TACK, YACK, COAL, COLA, CLAP, TALC, LACY, CLAY, COAT, TACO, CARP, CRAP, PACT

5-Letter Words:
CAULK, LAYUP, VAULT, BUILT, BULKY, BLURT, BURLY, CLUCK, LURCH, PLUCK, LUCKY, CLOUT, CURLY, TULIP, TRULY

6-Letter Words:
HUBCAP, BACKUP, CARHOP, PATCHY, PIRACY, PHOBIC, PUBLIC, OCCUPY

7-Letter Words:
BIVOUAC, VIBRATO, PRIVACY, PIVOTAL, VIRTUAL, VICTORY

PAGE 218
LAWYER, MILDEW, SWIVEL, BESTOW

ABSOLUTE, INBOUNDS, GOSLINGS

PAGE 219
VINEGAR, EPITAPH

PAGE 220

					B			
		F			R			
		L		D	O	Z	E	
		A			W			
		V			N			
		O			I			
	T	R	I	N	K	E	T	

PAGE 221

		T					
	A		Q				
	I		U		I		
	L		O		N		
P	O	U	R	E	D		
	R		U		I		
			M		G		
					O		

PAGE 222
AMPLIFY, MISPLAY, IMPALES, REALISM, MIRAGES, REGIMES, MERGERS, RESURGE

WROUGHT, TOUGHER, TOUCHER, OUTRACE, LOCATER, CALORIE, DECRIAL, MEDICAL

PAGE 223
DISSONANT,
TACTICIAN,
VENTILATE,
EMPHASIZE,
COLLEGIAN

PAGE 224
ROCKET,
TROLLEY,
ESCALATOR

PELICAN,
BITTERN,
CARDINAL

PAGE 225
ELEGANCE,
TABULATE,
ABNORMAL,
STUBBORN,
OBLIGATE

PAGE 226

```
1.  G
    L
  J A R S
    N   H
    D   R
        U S E R
        G

2.      H
      J U G S
        R
        L
  D A N G E R S
        R

3.          R
    D       A S H
    R       R
  J U N G L E S
    G

4.        A
          N
          G
          L
      R A Z E
  J U D G E R
    S       R S
```

PAGE 227

1.
```
      M
C R E E P
      T
      T
      L
  R E B E L
      E
```

2.
```
          E
          M
          B
  C       E
  R
L E T T E R
  P
  E L
```

3.
```
  T     E
B E L L
  M     E R E
  P     C
  E     T
  R
```

4.
```
  C
  R
  E
  E
  P
  T R E M B L E
  E         E
            L
            T
```

PAGE 228
GLUTTON,
GRAVITY,
INKBLOT,
BEATNIK,
PATRIOT,
POPULAR,
BIFOCAL,
ARRAIGN,
DUALITY,
ENVIRON,
ENTITLE,
LECTERN

PAGE 229
1-13, 2-7, 3-8, 4-10,
5-14, 6-11, 9-12

PAGES 230–231
Possible solutions:

4-Letter Words:
ABED, BADE,
BEAD, DEAD,
AGED, DEAN,
DARE, DEAR,
READ, DATE,
BEND, BODE,
BRED, DEBT,
DONE, NODE,
NERD, REND,
TEND, DENT,
DOER, REDO,
RODE, DOTE

5-Letter Words:
ABBOT, BATON,
TOTED, ATONE,
BEGOT, ORATE,
TANGO, TAROT,
DOTED, NOTED,
TONED, TENOR,
TONER, OTTER,
TORTE

6-Letter Words:
GADGET, TAGGED,
GRATED, GARNET,
GARTER, GRATER,
TARGET, GOTTEN

7-Letter Words:
BRANDED,
BONDAGE,
BROADEN,
BARTEND,
ADORNED,
DONATED

PAGE 232
ABSENCE,
BREATHE,
INHABIT,
NEWBORN

CREDITOR,
DISALLOW,
ANCHORED

PAGES 233
SUBLEASE,
SEATBELT

PAGE 234

```
              S
G O L F       O
        A R C H E R Y
              C
          T E N N I S
              R
```

PAGE 235

```
                  S
                  P
          R       L
N O R T H B O U N D
          Y       T
          T       C
          H       H
          M
```

PAGE 236
CRUMBLE,
TUMBLER,
BLUNTER,
TUNABLE,
NOTABLE,
TANGELO,
TONNAGE,
ATONING

VIBRATO,
OBVIATE,
VIOLATE,
ISOLATE,
LOCATES,
LATCHES,
LEACHES,
HECKLES

PAGE 237
CANDIDACY,
ARCHITECT,
COMBATANT,
DEMAGOGUE,
PALMISTRY

PAGE 238
SQUIRREL,
GORILLA,
PORPOISE

ARTICHOKE,

CASSEROLE,
CANTALOUPE

PAGE 239
CHAIRMAN,
DOWNBEAT,
MADHOUSE,
FESTIVAL,
SHOELACE

PAGE 240

1.
```
        K
  H     N
Z O M B I E
  T     V
      F E D
        S
```

2.
```
      F S
M   H I V E
D O Z E N   T
  B     K
```

3.
```
  M
  O       D
  V   F   E
Z E N I T H S
  B       K
```

4.
```
D
I F
T
Z   M
B E H O V E
S   N
    K
```

PAGE 241

1.
```
  J     T
K A Z O O
  W     U
        G
      H E M
        V
        E
```

2.
```
  J
Z O O M
    G A W K
    U
    V
  T H E E
```

3.
```
    H   M
    A V O W
    Z   T
J O K E   E
U
G
```

4.
```
    M     J
  V A G U E
    Z     T O
W O K E     H
```

PAGE 242
DAYLONG,
ASKANCE,
STANDBY,
STEALTH,
HANDBAG,
FISTFUL,
ABSTAIN,
MACRAME,
MAUDLIN,
MARITAL or
MARTIAL,
WARTIME,
SEASICK

PAGE 243
1-13, 2-14, 3-10,
4-9, 5-7, 6-11, 8-12

PAGES 244–245
Possible solutions:

4-Letter Words:
AIDE, IDEA,
DALE, DEAL,
LEAD, DEAN,
APED, DATE,
LANE, LEAN,
LEAP, PALE,
PLEA, PEAL,
LATE, TALE,
NAPE, NEAP,
PANE, ANTE,
NEAT, PATE,
PEAT, TAPE

5-Letter Words:
AILED, IDEAL,
PLAID, TIDAL,
ALIEN, PLAIN,
LINED, PILED,
PLIED, TILDE,
TILED, ELITE,
INLET, TITLE,
LIPID

6-Letter Words:
PATINA, ATTAIN,
DETAIL, DILATE,
TAILED, DETAIN,
ENTAIL, PLIANT

7-Letter Words:
TILAPIA,
DEPLANE,
PANELED,
PLEATED,
PAINTED,
PALETTE

PAGE 246
MARSHAL,
HEADFUL,
GINGHAM,
FISHNET

CREDIBLE,
DISTRICT,
MAINLAND

PAGE 247
MEMBRANE,
OCCUPANT

PAGE 248
IMPOUND,
PODIUMS,
IMPOSED,
PERIODS,
STEROID,
FORTIES,
SWIFTER,
FRETSAW

LIGHTER,
TINGLER,
ELATING,
TEAMING,
AMBIENT,
BOATMEN,
ABDOMEN,
BONDMAN

PAGE 249
DEFEATIST,
MENAGERIE,
REPAIRMEN,

PERSONAGE,
DISPUTANT

PAGE 250
MARIGOLD,
GOLDENROD,
DANDELION

CRIMSON,
LAVENDER,
CHARTREUSE

PAGE 251
MEDIEVAL,
RAILROAD,
GRATUITY,
SCAFFOLD,
DYNAMICS

PAGE 252

1.
```
          Z
R E C I T E
    U     E
    B
  D E A L T
```

2.
```
R E A L I Z E D
        C     E
        U     B
        T     T
        E
```

3.
```
      B
    R I T Z
    E
  E E
C L U E
  A   D
  T
  E
```

4.
```
C A T
L
U
B R E E Z E D
  I
  T
  E
```

PAGE 253

1.
```
        W
        O
        R I S K
        R
B E L L Y
U
R
P
```

282

2.
```
          B Y
      L   L
      U   I
      R   P
  W O R K E R S
```

3.
```
      P   R
  B L U R R Y
      O   E
      W
      L
      S K I
```

4.
```
      P       W
    B U R R O
      L       K
      L
  R I S E
      Y
```

PAGE 254
CALCIFY,
TRUSTEE,
RHOMBIC,
NEMESIS,
FORTUNE,
RAGGEDY,
NECKTIE,
SNOWMAN,
LIBRARY,
FANFARE,
PRONOUN,
DIVULGE

PAGE 255
1-7, 2-6, 3-12, 4-9, 5-14, 8-11, 10-13

PAGES 256–257
Possible solutions:

4-Letter Words:
CLOG, COIL, LOCI, COOL, LOCO, CLOP, CLOT, COLT, CLOY, FLOG, GOLF, FOIL, FOOL, FLOP, LOFT, FOUL, LOGO, LOGY, HOLY, LIMO, ROIL, LOOT, LOOP, POLO

5-Letter Words:
COUGH, LOGIC, CHOIR, CLOTH, MOOCH, POOCH, PORCH, POUCH, TORCH, COUTH, TOUCH, OPTIC, TOPIC, CURIO, COLOR

6-Letter Words:
FROLIC, FRIGHT, FORGOT, FOURTH, FROTHY, FIRMLY, PROFIT, PURIFY

7-Letter Words:
GROUCHY, COURTLY, OUTCROP, ROUGHLY, TURMOIL, POULTRY

PAGE 258
CAPTAIN,
CHEAPEN,
SCOURGE,
TRICEPS

CYCLONES,
SEAWARDS,
VAGRANTS

PAGE 259
DYNAMITE,
THOUSAND

PAGE 260
BALCONY,
BALONEY,
BLARNEY,
BLANDER,
DANGLER,
READING,
GAUDIER,
FIGURED

THEREIN,
TRAINEE,
RETAINS,
ENTAILS,
DENIALS,
SUNDIAL,
UPLANDS,
UPLOADS

PAGE 261
BAPTISMAL,
NAIVETIES,
SATELLITE,
BUNGALOWS,
SACRIFICE

PAGE 262
HAMSTER,
PANTHER,
STALLION

INCISOR,
EARLOBE,
PANCREAS

PAGE 263
SPOILAGE,
UNEASILY,
ANYPLACE,
PANORAMA,
DAYLIGHT

PAGE 264

1.
```
          S
          I
          G
        C H I
    V   U
  B O O R
  W     I
        O
```

2.
```
          H I
      B   O
      I   U
  V I G O R
        S C O W
```

3.
```
          B
          O
  V I C I O U S
    R     G
    O     H I
    W
```

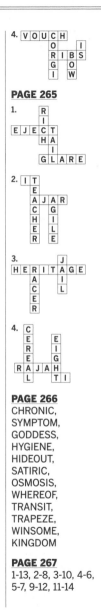

4.
```
  V O U C H
      O       I
      R I B S
      G   O
      I   W
```

PAGE 265

1.
```
        R
        I
  E J E C T
        H A
        I
        G L A R E
```

2.
```
  I T
  E
  A J A R
  C   G
  H   I
  E   L
  R   E
```

3.
```
          J
  H E R I T A G E
        A   I
        C   L
        E
        R
```

4.
```
  C
  E       E
  R       I
  E       G
  R A J A H
  L       T I
```

PAGE 266
CHRONIC,
SYMPTOM,
GODDESS,
HYGIENE,
HIDEOUT,
SATIRIC,
OSMOSIS,
WHEREOF,
TRANSIT,
TRAPEZE,
WINSOME,
KINGDOM

PAGE 267
1-13, 2-8, 3-10, 4-6, 5-7, 9-12, 11-14

THE AUTHORS

JOE EDLEY

Joe Edley lives for word games. In addition to being a master Bananagrammer, he is also the only three-time National Scrabble Champion (1980, 1992, 2000). Since 1988 he's been the Director of Clubs and Tournaments for the National Scrabble Association. In that role, he has created thousands of word puzzles to entertain the readers of *The Scrabble News*. Joe also writes a syndicated newspaper column, "Scrabblegrams," and teaches at Scrabble events across the country. He lives with his family on Long Island, New York.

BANANAGRAMS

Bananagrams is a family company. Abe Nathanson, along with his daughter Rena and his grandchildren Aaron and Ava, invented the game while spending the summer of 2005 together in Narragansett, Rhode Island. They soon decided—after some encouragement from friends—to try selling it. It debuted at the 2006 London Toy Fair and quickly became an international sensation. The whole family is actively involved in the growing company. They live in the UK and in Providence, Rhode Island, where Abe runs the office.